CHOWDERLAND

CHOWDERLAND

HEARTY SOUPS & STEWS

with Sides & Salads to Match

BROOKE DOJNY

Photography by Keller + Keller

Storey Publishing

The mission of Storey Publishing is to serve our customers by
publishing practical information that encourages
personal independence in harmony with the environment.

Edited by Margaret Sutherland and Sarah Guare
Art direction by Jessica Armstrong
Cover and interior design by Jackie Lay
Indexed by Christine R. Lindemer, Boston Road Communications

Illustrations and hand lettering throughout by Jackie Lay
Cover and interior photography by © Keller + Keller Photography, except
   © Bruce Block/Getty Images, 53; Richard Dojny, back cover (author);
   © Lisa Fletcher/Getty Images, 65; © Michael Powell/Getty Images, 57;
   © Paul Poplis/Getty Images, 127; © Robbie George/Getty Images, 115
Food styling by Catrine Kelty

Storey Publishing
210 MASS MoCA Way
North Adams, MA 01247
www.storey.com

Printed in China by R.R. Donnelley
10   9   8   7   6   5   4   3   2   1

LIBRARY OF CONGRESS CATALOGING-IN-PUBLICATION DATA

Dojny, Brooke.
  Chowderland : hearty soups & stews with sides & salads to match / by Brooke Dojny.
     pages cm
  Includes index.
  ISBN 978-1-61212-375-2 (hardcover with jacket : alk. paper)
  ISBN 978-1-61212-376-9 (ebook) 1. Soups. 2. Stews. 3. Side dishes (Cooking) I. Title.
TX757.D65 2015
641.81′3—dc23
                    2014043278

For Holly, Morgan, and Thompson

ACKNOWLEDGMENTS

Thank you to the following people who helped immensely with thinking, providing historical background, cooking, and tasting: Melanie Barnard, Donna and Marston Brewer, Beth Bunker, David Chalfant, Phyllis Corcoran, Matt Dojny, Maury Dojny, Richard Dojny, Sarah and Tony Everdell, Patti and Floyd Gelini, Tad and Lindsay Goodale, Lee and Don Holmes, Sally Jennings, Charmaine Jensen, Barbara and Prep Keyes, Susan Maloney, Sandy Oliver, Carol and Peter Osgood, Nancy and Jimmy Reinish, Nancy Sandreuter, Bill and Joy Schmitt, Pam and Ralph Siewers, Veronica and Michael Stubbs, Jasper White, and Sybil Young. And very special thanks to Martha Maury Welty for her excellent testing.

I'm grateful, as always, to my agent, Judith Weber, and to all the wonderfully talented staff at Storey Publishing — amazing editors, designers, photographers and publicists. Thank you, especially, to Margaret Sutherland, Matt LaBombard, and Sarah Guare.

CONTENTS

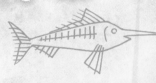

CHOW

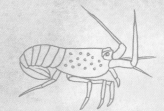

DERLAND

WELCOME to CHOWDERLAND

Chowder — mostly seafood but sometimes with just vegetables or chicken or a combination thereof — is an old European/North American dish that has traveled with us for hundreds of years, yet it emerges into the twenty-first century more popular than ever. Relatively small amounts of animal protein (or none at all) paired with potatoes, onions, other vegetables, and broth or milk result in the kind of simple-to-make, delicious, and sustainable one-pot dish that we love to eat today.

Much lore, history, and myth surround the subject of chowder — its origins, its place in literary history, and its evolution from shipboard fare thickened with ship's biscuit to today's versions that are typically bound with flour or the starchiness of potatoes. Chowder's origins remain shrouded in mystery, but food historians agree that it evolved aboard French and English fishing boats and in the Nova Scotia and New England coastal communities where fishermen settled. The word is probably from *chaudière*, the French term for the cauldron in which fishermen cooked their chowders. The first American cookbook to include a chowder recipe was the 1800 edition of Amelia Simmons's *American Cookery*, which listed the ingredients as "bass, salt pork, crackers, and a side dish of potatoes." By the 1840s, potatoes had become a standard chowder ingredient, eventually replacing crackers altogether.

Chowder moved along with the westward expansion, incorporating indigenous ingredients along the way, including chopped Pismo clams in California, geoducks along the

Oregon coast, and salmon in the Northwest. San Franciscans hollow out round loaves of sourdough bread to use as an edible bowl for chowder.

Chowder began as a fish soup, but, as with many things culinary, the dish has evolved and broadened over the years. Since I must come up with some sort of chowder definition, here it is: a chunky, hearty soup, usually made with salt pork or bacon, onions, potatoes, the main ingredient (often seafood), and a liquid. That's the starting point. From there, home cooks and chefs add or subtract — leaving out the pork to create a meatless brew, replacing onions with leeks or garlic, switching up the liquid — with potatoes as a constant.

Potatoes

Potatoes are a crucial ingredient in chowders, and I specify which type to use in each recipe. Most recipes call for a floury potato, such as all-purpose or Yukon Gold, that releases starch and helps thicken the chowder. Some recipes call for red-skinned potatoes, which I like in more delicate chowders. The chowders that use these less-starchy potatoes often include a little flour to boost their thickening power.

To dice or slice potatoes, I recommend the Japanese chef's knife called Santoku. It has grooves that allow for better separation between blade and potato — hence, less sticking.

Salt Pork and Bacon

Most chowder recipes begin with rendering ("trying out" is the old-fashioned term) diced salt pork or bacon, removing the cooked bits for adding back later, and using the full-of-flavor fat to continue building the chowder. Salt pork and bacon can almost always be used interchangeably, but each recipe in this book will specify one or the other — or either. Salt pork was the early American cook's basic cooking fat and also served as seasoning, accenting chowders with its incomparably rich, salty flavor. In recipes for very traditional chowders (Boston-Style Creamy Clam Chowder, for instance; see page 9), I call for salt pork *or* bacon, putting the salt pork first to indicate my preference; others call only for bacon.

CHOWDER ORATOR
American statesman and orator Daniel Webster was considered an authority on chowders. He once delivered a lengthy speech on the floor of the U.S. Senate about the virtues of chowder.

Some chefs insist on making chowder with applewood-smoked or at least thick-sliced slab bacon. I call for just plain bacon because I think the standard commercial product is fine, but if you happen to have special artisan bacon, so much the better.

Salt pork is usually available in the cured meats section of the supermarket. The first thing you need to do with salt pork is slice off the thick rind. Presliced salt pork makes dicing easier, especially if the pork is slightly frozen first. You can also cut the pork into chunks and pulse in a food processor to finely chop it. Modern salt pork seldom releases much fat, so it is usually cooked with additional butter. After browning and removing salt pork or bacon bits from the pot, pour the rendered fat into a glass measure to check the quantity, or simply estimate the quantity visually.

Crackers

Early chowders were thickened and bound with a very hard, flat cracker called ship's biscuit, or hardtack. In the 1800s ship's biscuit was replaced by potatoes, and crackers moved to the side as an accompaniment. A bowl of restaurant chowder almost always comes with a little packet of small, plain, crunchy oyster crackers, which can be sprinkled over the chowder or eaten on the side. Nabisco's Crown Pilot crackers, which were the direct descendant of hardtack ship's biscuit and every chowder aficionado's cracker of choice, were discontinued several years ago. Vermont-made common crackers or saltines are good substitutes.

Which Pot?

Size matters, but even more important is the pot's material. I begin almost every chowder recipe with the words "Cook the salt pork or bacon in a large heavy soup pot or Dutch oven over medium-low heat." You can use a pot of almost any material — enamel-clad cast iron, heavy aluminum, stainless-clad aluminum — as long as the pot is heavy gauge. Flimsy, thin cookware (such as speckled tin, steel canning kettles, or even some thin-walled stockpots) heats unevenly, and bacon or salt pork will burn, onions will scorch, and,

CHATHAM PIER FISH MARKET

ENTRANCE

most crucially, heated milk or cream can curdle. Dutch ovens are thick-walled pots with tight-fitting lids, such as the enamel-coated cast-iron cookware made by Le Creuset.

When making a chowder for four to six people, a 5- to 6-quart pot will be sufficient; chowder or seafood stew for six to eight people should be made in a 6- to 8-quart pot. Chowder is great party food; if you don't have a pot large enough to serve a crowd, use two smaller pots.

Clam Juice and Seafood Broth

If possible, I call for a cooking method that incorporates broth-making as part of a chowder or seafood stew recipe, but when that is not practical, I'll often suggest bottled clam juice or purchased seafood broth as an alternative. (Since there is no official culinary differentiation between broth and stock, I have chosen the term "broth" in this book.) Bottled clam juice is usually shelved with the tuna and other canned seafood. Look for seafood broth — in cans or shelf-stable cartons, or in jars as a concentrate — with the canned chicken and beef broth. I haven't made much mention of fish stock, because fish frames (bones and trimmings) aren't easy to find these days. However, if you're lucky enough to have a whole fish, simply break up the frames, cover with water, add a teaspoon or so of salt, simmer for about 30 minutes, and strain.

Curing

Much flowery and amusing prose has been penned to emphasize the crucial importance of curing or aging chowders. "Aging," wrote New England author Robert P. Tristram Coffin, "brings out flavor no spices or sudden terrific heat can reach." Martha's Vineyard's newspaper of record, the *Vineyard Gazette*, once stated, "On the back of the stove is where much of the perfection comes in." It's not that uncured chowder is a bad thing; it's just that some aging — at least a couple of hours or up to a day or two — allows the flavors of the seafood and broth to meld and marry with the potatoes and other liquid, elevating the dish from very good to . . . supernal.

Each recipe provides directions for aging, but in general, if you are not serving the chowder within a couple of hours, refrigerate it *uncovered* until cold; then cover the pot.

Curdling

Most of the recipes in this book are curdle-proof, as long as you use full-fat (not skim or low-fat) fresh milk or cream. Check sell-by dates and don't buy a product if it's close to its expiration date. In general, if a recipe calls for milk or half-and-half, I use a bit of flour to stabilize the chowder to prevent curdling. If unthickened liquid is the desired result, I usually use heavy cream (which rarely curdles if fresh) in combination with broth or other liquid. Also, try to keep chowder from reaching a rolling boil, since this can destabilize the milk or cream.

If a chowder does curdle (or "break" or "split"), don't despair, for although it looks unpleasant, the chowder is perfectly safe to eat. Simply strain out the solids, whir the liquid in a blender to pull it back together, and reheat over very low heat.

Freezing?

Most chowders or seafood stews, with the notable exception of Bermuda Fish Chowder (see page 32), don't freeze particularly well. The potatoes, especially, tend to get mushy and break down, and the flavors of the chowder become somewhat muted. Frozen chowder is usually perfectly edible, but if you need to freeze it, do try to eat it within a week or two.

NEWPORT'S CHOWDER FEST
Newport, Rhode Island, has been staging its Chowder Cook-Off for almost 35 years, with chefs and other food professionals from all over the country competing for "Best Clam," "Best Seafood," and "Best Creative" chowder. The annual festival draws thousands of enthusiastic chowder-happy eaters.

1 The CHOWDER POT

BOSTON-STYLE CREAMY CLAM CHOWDER

- 4 ounces salt pork or bacon, cut into ½-inch dice or ground in the food processor (about 1 cup) (see Notes)
- 6 tablespoons butter, plus more if needed
- 1 large onion, chopped
- 1 large celery stalk, thinly sliced
- 3 tablespoons all-purpose flour
- 3 cups bottled clam juice (see Notes)
- 2 cups water, plus more if needed
- 1 pound all-purpose potatoes, peeled and diced (about 3 cups)
- 2 teaspoons dried thyme or 2 tablespoons chopped fresh (see Notes)
- 1 bay leaf, broken in half
- 3 cups chopped hard-shell clams with their liquor (see Notes)
- 1½ cups heavy cream
  Salt and freshly ground black pepper
- 3 tablespoons chopped flat-leaf parsley

This chowder, made with hard-shell clams and lightly flour-thickened, originated in the Boston area and over time has become the chowder standard for most of the country. It is a rich, creamy, deeply flavorful brew, plain and unadorned, except for the scatter of thyme and fresh parsley. Pass a bowl of traditional oyster crackers and add Vinegary Cabbage Slaw (page 105) and Dark and Sticky Candied Gingerbread (page 129) for a terrific any-season supper.

4–5 SERVINGS

1. Cook the salt pork with the butter in a large heavy soup pot or Dutch oven over medium-low heat until crisp and the fat is rendered, 10 to 15 minutes. Remove the cooked bits with a slotted spoon, drain on paper towels, and reserve. If you don't have 8 tablespoons of fat in the pot, make up the difference with additional butter.

2. Add the onion and celery and cook over medium heat until they begin to soften, about 5 minutes. Sprinkle on the flour and cook, stirring, for 2 minutes. Add the clam juice and water and bring to a boil over high heat, whisking until smooth.

3. Add the potatoes, thyme, and bay leaf, and cook, covered, over medium-low heat until the potatoes are tender, about →

15 minutes. Add the clams and cream, cook for 5 minutes, and remove from the heat. Season with salt and pepper to taste. Let the chowder sit at cool room temperature for at least an hour or, better yet, refrigerate for up to 2 days.

4. Reheat over low heat, adding more broth, cream, or water if the chowder is too thick. Ladle into bowls, sprinkle with parsley, and pass the reserved pork bits (reheated in the microwave) for sprinkling on the chowder if desired.

NOTES

If you're using bacon it should produce enough of its own fat, so there's no need to cook it in butter. After removing the cooked bits, you should have about 2 tablespoons of bacon fat; discard any excess and add 6 tablespoons butter to make a total of 8 tablespoons fat.

For this classic chowder, dried thyme is more traditional than fresh, but feel free to use either.

If you have fresh clams, scrub 5 to 6 pounds and steam them in 4 cups of water just until they open, 5 to 10 minutes. Then scrape out the clam meat and chop into pea-size pieces. Pour the cooking liquid into a glass measuring cup, let any sediment settle, and pour off 3 cups of the clean broth to use in place of the bottled clam juice.

Chopped hard-shell clams (with their liquor) can be found fresh or frozen in the seafood section of most supermarkets. Bottled clam juice is usually shelved with the canned fish in the supermarket.

ISHMAEL'S CHOWDER

"But when that smoking chowder came in, the mystery was delightfully explained. Oh, sweet friends! Hearken to me. It was made of small juicy clams, scarcely bigger than hazelnuts, mixed with pounded ship's biscuit, and salted pork cut up into little flakes; the whole enriched with butter, and plentifully seasoned with pepper and salt. Our appetites being sharpened by the frosty voyage, and in particular, Queequeg seeing his favorite fishy food before him, and the chowder being surpassingly excellent, we dispatched it with great expedition."
— Herman Melville, *Moby Dick*

CONNECTICUT SHORELINE
SEMI-CLEAR
CLAM CHOWDER

This is typical of the old-fashioned chowders they "build" along the Connecticut shoreline — untouched by flour, *mostly* clear broth, but with the addition of just enough evaporated milk to tame the rough edges of the chowder. Brussels Sprout Slaw (page 100) or purchased creamy coleslaw is a good accompaniment, along with oyster crackers and a plate of Spiced Hermit Bar Cookies (page 131) to finish.

4 SERVINGS

4 ounces salt pork or bacon, cut into ½-inch dice or ground in the food processor (about 1 cup) (see Notes)

2 tablespoons butter, plus more if needed

1 medium onion, chopped

1 celery stalk, chopped

2 cups bottled clam juice or broth from cooked clams (see Notes)

2 cups water

1 pound all-purpose potatoes, peeled and diced (about 3 cups)

2 cups chopped hard-shell clams with their liquor (see Notes)

½ cup evaporated milk

Salt and freshly ground black pepper

1. Cook the salt pork with the butter in a large heavy soup pot or Dutch oven over medium-low heat until crisp and the fat is rendered, 10 to 15 minutes. Remove the cooked bits with a slotted spoon, drain on paper towels, and reserve. If you don't have 4 tablespoons of fat in the pot, make up the difference with additional butter.

2. Add the onion and celery and cook over medium heat until they begin to soften, about 5 minutes. Add the clam juice, water, and potatoes, and bring to a boil. Reduce the heat to medium-low and cook, covered, until the potatoes are almost tender, about 10 minutes.

3. Add the clams with their liquor and cook until the potatoes are very tender, about 5 minutes longer. Stir in the evaporated milk and heat gently. (Try not to boil or the chowder could curdle.) Season with salt and pepper to taste. Let the chowder sit for at least an hour at cool room temperature or, better yet, refrigerate for up to 2 days. →

4. Reheat over low heat, ladle into bowls, and pass the reserved pork bits (reheated in the microwave) for sprinkling on the chowder if desired.

NOTES

If you're using bacon it should produce enough of its own fat, so there's no need to cook it in butter. After removing the cooked bits, you should have about 2 tablespoons of bacon fat; discard any excess and add 2 tablespoons butter to make a total of 4 table-spoons fat.

To use fresh clams, scrub 4 pounds clams and steam them in 4 cups of water just until they open, 5 to 10 minutes. Then scrape out the clam meat and chop into pea-size pieces. Pour the cooking liquid into a glass measuring cup, let any sediment settle, and pour off 3 cups of the clean broth to use in the chowder in place of the bottled clam juice and clam liquor.

Bottled clam juice is usually shelved with the canned fish in the supermarket. Clam "liquor" is the sweet, flavorful liquid inside a raw clam. Chopped fresh or frozen hard-shell clams are packed in their liquor, and it should definitely be added to any chowder.

> **CLAM-DIGGING MEMORIES**
>
> "My grandfather delivered vegetables and fresh fish in Portland, Maine, and every Saturday I dug clams with my dad on the Nonesuch River in Scarborough. We dug rain or shine — and believe me, we were out there in some pretty rough weather."
>
> — Nancy Sandreuter, Winchester, Massachusetts

ABOUT CLAMS

All clams are either hard-shell or soft-shell, and within each category, the smaller clams are more tender than the larger. The smallest hard-shells, such as littlenecks, which are usually less than 2 inches across, are highly prized for eating raw (on the half shell) or for cooking. The largest hard-shells, which run from 3 to 6 inches across, are called quahogs (pronounced koh-hogs) or chowder clams and are best chopped and used in chowders. Soft-shells — also called steamers because that is the way they're usually cooked — are also more desirable if they are not huge, although they can be cut into pieces for chowder if necessary.

There are several varieties of Pacific clams. Hard-shells include butter clams, Pismo clams, and Manila clams. Geoduck and razor clams are examples of Pacific soft-shells.

BUYING

Clams must be alive when you buy them. Hard-shells are shut up quite tight, and if they're dead, you can move their shells apart. Live soft-shells react visibly when touched, retracting their necks and closing more tightly — although they're never closed all the way, hence the name "gapers."

STORING

Don't store clams in sealed plastic or in fresh water. Just put them in a bowl and store in the coldest part of the refrigerator, where they should stay alive for several days — although the sooner you cook and eat them, the better.

CLEANING

Hard-shell clams require only a quick scrub with a stiff brush. Soft-shells often contain sand or mud. Jasper White, a noted Boston chef, recommends soaking steamer clams in big bowls of cold salted water for several hours, gently lifting them from one bowl to the other, changing and swishing the water and repeating the process until the water is almost clear of any sediment.

milky maine
STEAMER CHOWDER

This is the archetypal Maine clam chowder, made with sweet briny steamer clams and containing nary a trace of flour thickener. "Flour in chowder," says noted Portland chef Sam Hayward of Fore Street, "is anathema in Maine." Instead, the chowder derives some body from the starch released by the floury potatoes. Its creaminess comes from evaporated milk, which was originally used for its convenience but has now become fairly standard in many traditional recipes. Serve with Crusty Skillet Cornbread (page 89) or oyster crackers and Brussels Sprout Slaw (page 100).

4 SERVINGS

- 4 pounds small to medium-size soft-shell clams (about 50 clams)
- 5 cups water
- 4 ounces salt pork or bacon, chopped into ½-inch dice or ground in the food processor (about 1 cup) (see Note)
- 4 tablespoons butter, plus more if needed
- 1 large onion, chopped
- 1½ pounds all-purpose potatoes, peeled and diced (about 4½ cups)
- 2 cups evaporated milk
- Salt and freshly ground black pepper

1. Scrub the clams well and rinse in several changes of water if they are muddy. (See About Clams, page 13.) Bring the water to a boil in a large pot and add the clams. Return to a boil, then reduce the heat to medium-low. Cook, covered, shaking the pot a couple of times to redistribute the clams, until they open, about 5 minutes. Use a slotted spoon to transfer the clams to a bowl. Pour the clam broth into another bowl, leaving any sediment behind.

2. Working over the bowl to catch juices, remove the clams from their shells. Pull off the black skin and snip off the black necks if you don't like the looks of them in your chowder. Cut the clams with a large knife or scissors into approximately ¾-inch pieces and set them aside. Let the broth stand for at least 30 minutes, then measure out 5 cups, leaving any additional black sediment behind. (The clams and broth can be prepared a day ahead. Cover and refrigerate.)

3. Cook the salt pork with the butter in a large heavy soup pot or Dutch oven over medium-low heat until crisp and the

fat is rendered, 10 to 15 minutes. Remove the cooked bits with a slotted spoon, drain on paper towels, and reserve. If you don't have 6 tablespoons of fat in the pot, make up the difference with additional butter.

4. Add the onion and cook over medium heat until it begins to soften, about 5 minutes. Add the 5 cups clam broth and the diced potatoes, bring to a boil, then reduce the heat to medium-low. Cook, covered, until the potatoes are tender, about 15 minutes.

5. Add the cooked clams, stir in the evaporated milk, and heat through over gentle heat. (Try not to boil or the chowder could curdle.) Season with salt and pepper to taste. Let the chowder sit for at least an hour at cool room temperature or, better yet, refrigerate for up to 2 days.

6. Reheat over very low heat, stirring frequently, until the chowder steams and is heated through. Ladle into bowls and pass the reserved pork bits (reheated in the microwave) for sprinkling on the chowder if desired.

NOTE

If you're using bacon it should produce enough of its own fat, so there's no need to cook it in butter. After removing the cooked bits, you should have about 2 tablespoons of bacon fat; discard any excess and add 4 tablespoons butter to make a total of 6 tablespoons fat.

MANHATTAN-STYLE CLAM CHOWDER

4 ounces bacon, cut into ½-inch pieces (about 1 cup)

2 tablespoons olive oil

1 large onion, chopped

2 celery stalks, chopped

1 small green bell pepper, seeded and chopped

2 carrots, cut into ½-inch dice

2 garlic cloves, finely chopped

1 (14½-ounce) can diced tomatoes in juice

3 cups bottled clam juice (see Note)

1 cup water

1 pound all-purpose potatoes, peeled and diced (about 3 cups)

¾ teaspoon salt, plus more if needed

2 teaspoons dried oregano

1 bay leaf, broken in half

2 cups chopped hard-shell clams with their liquor

3 tablespoons chopped flat-leaf parsley

Freshly ground black pepper

As a New Englander born and bred, I've always been somewhat resistant to Manhattan-style chowder, which is made with various vegetables, including tomatoes. Oh, heresy, Connecticut and Massachusetts folks would cry! But, truth to tell, it's a really delicious soup — er, chowder — especially when served with a basket of warm Rosemary-Onion Focaccia (page 93).

4 SERVINGS

1. Cook the bacon in a large heavy soup pot or Dutch oven over medium-low heat until crisp and the fat is rendered, 10 to 15 minutes. Remove the cooked bits with a slotted spoon, drain on paper towels, and reserve. You should have 2 tablespoons of fat in the pot; if there is too much, pour some off, or if there is too little, make up the difference with additional olive oil.

2. Add the oil to the pot and cook the onion, celery, bell pepper, carrots, and garlic over medium heat until they soften, about 8 minutes. Add the tomatoes, clam juice, and water to the pot, along with the diced potatoes, salt, oregano, and bay leaf. Bring to a boil, then reduce the heat to medium-low and cook, covered, until the potatoes are almost tender, about 15 minutes. (The tomatoes will slow the cooking time of the potatoes, so you may need to cook a few extra minutes.)

3. Add the clams with their liquor and cook until the potatoes are very tender, about 5 minutes longer. Stir in the reserved bacon and the parsley and season with pepper and additional salt if needed. Let the chowder sit for at least an hour at cool room temperature or, better yet, refrigerate for up to 2 days.

4. Reheat over low heat, ladle into bowls, and serve.

NOTE
Bottled clam juice is usually shelved with the canned fish in the supermarket.

MANHATTAN CHOWDER THEORIES

Manhattan clam chowder — a clear broth with tomatoes and other vegetables — can be traced back to the 1890s, when it seems to have been called Fulton Fish Market clam chowder or New York clam chowder. One theory is that Manhattan clam chowder originated with Neapolitan immigrants, who adapted their *zuppa di vongole* to New World ingredients. Others posit that the addition of tomatoes in place of milk was initially the work of Portuguese immigrants in Rhode Island. Scornful New Englanders called this version Manhattan-style clam chowder because, in their view, any name attached to New York was an insult.

ROCKY POINT RED CHOWDER

If you type "Rocky Point chowder" into any search engine, you will get dozens and dozens of postings from rabidly nostalgic people waxing rhapsodic about the red chowder and clam cakes that were served at Rocky Point Amusement Park in Warwick, Rhode Island, from about the 1920s through the 1950s. Although the park is long closed, the chowder lives on in the memories of those who loved it. This recipe is a composite of what I found in my research.

The tomato soup is authentic and adds not just color and flavor but also some thickening power and a touch of sweetness. This chowder is especially great with Narragansett Clam Fritters (page 87), of course.

4 SERVINGS

4 ounces salt pork or bacon, cut into ½-inch dice or ground in the food processor (about 1 cup) (see Notes)

3 tablespoons butter, plus more if needed

1 large onion, chopped

2 cups bottled clam juice (see Notes)

3 cups water

1¼ pounds all-purpose potatoes, peeled and diced (about 3¾ cups)

1 teaspoon Old Bay Seasoning

3 cups chopped hard-shell clams with their liquor (see Notes)

¾ cup condensed tomato soup

1½ teaspoons paprika

Salt and freshly ground black pepper

1. Cook the salt pork with the butter in a large heavy soup pot or Dutch oven over medium-low heat until crisp and the fat is rendered, 10 to 15 minutes. Remove the cooked bits with a slotted spoon, drain on paper towels, and reserve. If you don't have 5 tablespoons of fat in the pot, make up the difference with additional butter.

2. Add the onion and cook over medium heat until it begins to soften, about 5 minutes. Add the clam juice, water, potatoes, and Old Bay. Bring to a boil, then reduce the heat to medium-low and cook, uncovered, until the potatoes are tender, about 15 minutes.

3. Add the clams, tomato soup, and paprika, and cook for 5 minutes. Season with salt and pepper to taste (since the clams, clam juice, and tomato soup are salty, the chowder may not need more salt). Let the chowder sit at cool room temperature for at least an hour or, better yet, refrigerate for up to 2 days.

4. Reheat over low heat, ladle into bowls, and pass the reserved pork bits (reheated in the microwave) for sprinkling on the chowder if desired.

NOTES

If you're using bacon it should produce enough of its own fat, so there's no need to cook it in butter. After removing the cooked bits, you should have about 2 tablespoons of bacon fat; discard any excess and add 3 tablespoons butter to make a total of 5 tablespoons fat.

Bottled clam juice is usually shelved with the canned fish in the supermarket.

Chopped hard-shell clams can be found fresh or frozen in the seafood section of most supermarkets.

REGIONAL CLAM CHOWDER WARS

Clam chowders differ as to the type of clams used, the choice of liquid, the decision to thicken with flour or not, and the use of salt pork or bacon.

In Maine, chowder was always made with soft-shell clams ("steamers") because hard-shell clams (also called quahogs) were rare in the state. Traditional Maine chowder is milky and brothy, thickened only by the starch released by potatoes.

Classic Boston-style chowder is made with chopped hard-shell clams and milk or cream, and it is thickened with some flour.

In Connecticut and some parts of Rhode Island, traditional chowder is "clear," that is, made with clam broth and with little or no milk.

Some Rhode Islanders add chopped tomatoes to their chowder — a subject that can stir heated debate.

Manhattan chowder is akin to vegetable soup with chopped hard-shell clams added.

CLASSIC RHODE ISLAND
CLEAR CLAM CHOWDER

Three types of chowder are listed on many menus in Rhode Island — red, creamy, and clear. Clear is by far the most traditional and is still the preference of most local people, especially when balanced by a nice greasy clam fritter served alongside. In fact, this chowder probably dates way back — maybe even to the late eighteenth century — before potatoes showed up in New England and chowders were thickened with ship's biscuit.

This is a primal and austere brew, beautiful in its honest plainness. It speaks to the historical continuity of chowder and should be served with those fritters (page 87), oyster crackers, or toasted common crackers.

4 SERVINGS

4 pounds hard-shell clams, any size, scrubbed (see Notes)

4 cups water

4 ounces salt pork or bacon, cut into ½-inch dice or ground in the food processor (about 1 cup) (see Notes)

2 tablespoons butter, plus more if needed

1 large onion, chopped

1 celery stalk, chopped

1 pound all-purpose potatoes, peeled and diced (about 3 cups)

2 teaspoons dried thyme or 2 tablespoons chopped fresh

Salt and freshly ground black pepper

1. Combine the clams and water in a large pot. Bring to a boil, then reduce the heat to medium. Cook, covered, shaking the pot a couple of times to redistribute the clams, until they open, 5 to 10 minutes. Use a slotted spoon to transfer the clams to a bowl. Pour the clam broth into another bowl, leaving any sediment behind. Remove the clams from their shells and chop into pea-size pieces. Measure out 4 cups of the broth.

2. Cook the salt pork with the butter in a large heavy soup pot or Dutch oven over medium-low heat until crisp and the fat is rendered, 10 to 15 minutes. Remove the cooked bits with a slotted spoon, drain on paper towels, and reserve. If you don't have 4 tablespoons of fat in the pot, make up the difference with additional butter.

3. Add the onion and celery and cook over medium heat until they begin to soften, about 5 minutes. Add the 4 cups reserved clam broth, potatoes, and thyme, and bring to a boil. Reduce the heat to medium-low and cook, covered, until the potatoes are almost tender, about 10 minutes. ⟶

4. Add the cooked clams and cook until the potatoes are very tender, about 5 minutes longer. Season with salt and pepper to taste. Let the chowder sit for at least an hour at cool room temperature or, better yet, refrigerate for up to 2 days.

5. Reheat over low heat, ladle into bowls, and pass the reserved pork bits (reheated in the microwave) for sprinkling on the chowder if desired.

NOTES

You could also use 4 cups bottled clam juice, or 2 cups clam juice and 2 cups water, and 2 cups chopped hard-shell clams (with their liquor), which can be found fresh or frozen in the seafood section of most supermarkets.

If you're using bacon it should produce enough of its own fat, so there's no need to cook it in butter. After removing the cooked bits, you should have about 2 tablespoons of bacon fat; discard any excess and add 2 tablespoons butter to make a total of 4 table-spoons fat.

RHODE ISLANDERS KNOW

"We go through a lot of clam cakes; I'd say we probably sell almost 60 dozen clam cakes a day. Rhode Islanders know what they want. They want their chowder and clam cakes."

— Amanda Maybeck, Champlin's Seafood, Narragansett, Rhode Island

The Chowder Pot   23

SPRING'S FIRST CHOWDER
with FRESH HERBS and PEAS

4 ounces bacon, cut into ½-inch pieces (about 1 cup)

2 tablespoons butter, plus more if needed

1 large onion, chopped

1 cup bottled clam juice or seafood broth (see Notes)

2 cups water

1 pound red-skinned potatoes, unpeeled and diced (about 3 cups)

3 slender young carrots, thinly sliced

¾ teaspoon salt, plus more if needed

1 cup heavy cream

1 pound haddock or other mild flaky fish fillets, cut into 4-inch chunks

1 cup fresh or frozen peas (see Notes)

½ cup snipped chives or thinly sliced scallions

2 tablespoons coarsely chopped dill

2 tablespoons coarsely chopped flat-leaf parsley

2 teaspoons coarsely chopped tarragon

Freshly ground black pepper

This lovely, delicate fish chowder is based on one from *The Four Season Farm Gardener's Cookbook* by Barbara Damrosch and Eliot Coleman. It uses not only spring's first tender carrots and peas (if you can't find fresh peas in pods, frozen are fine) but also copious amounts of fresh green herbs, chopped coarsely so they show off their beauty. Serve with a Bibb lettuce salad dressed with lemon vinaigrette, a basket of Red Pepper–Scallion Pita Toasts (page 91), and Strawberry-Rhubarb Cobbler (page 124) to finish.

4 SERVINGS

1. Cook the bacon in a large heavy soup pot or Dutch oven over medium-low heat until crisp and the fat is rendered, 10 to 15 minutes. Remove the cooked bits with a slotted spoon, drain on paper towels, and reserve. You should have 2 tablespoons of fat in the pot; if there is too much, pour some off, or if there is too little, make up the difference with additional butter.

2. Add the butter to the pot and cook the onion over medium heat until it begins to soften, about 5 minutes. Add the clam juice, water, potatoes, carrots, and salt, and bring to a boil. Reduce the heat to medium-low and cook, covered, until the potatoes and carrots are almost tender, about 12 minutes.

3. Add the cream and fish, bring to a simmer over medium heat, and cook until the fish is opaque, about 5 minutes. The fish will break apart as it cooks. →

4. Add the peas, chives, dill, parsley, and tarragon, and cook for 5 minutes if using fresh peas or about 2 minutes for frozen peas. Stir in the reserved bacon bits and season with pepper and additional salt if needed. Let the chowder sit at cool room temperature for at least an hour or refrigerate overnight.

5. Reheat over low heat, ladle into bowls, and serve.

NOTES

Bottled clam juice is usually shelved with the canned fish in the supermarket; seafood broth — in cans or shelf-stable cartons, or in jars as a concentrate — can usually be found with the canned chicken and beef broth.

If making the chowder a day ahead, add the peas and fresh herbs when reheating, since they will lose color upon standing.

ABOUT FISH

The nose tells all. A well-run fish market or seafood section of a supermarket will smell more like the ocean than fish. Fresh fish should have almost no odor. Fillets should be bright and shiny and the flesh should feel plump and firm to the touch, not mushy or soggy.

Lobster meat, crabmeat, scallops, and fish fillets or steaks can be stored overnight. Seal the seafood in a ziplock bag and place the bag in a bowl with enough ice cubes to surround the bag. Place in the coldest part of the refrigerator — usually the lowest part.

Seafood can be frozen for a week or two. Place small portions of fish fillets in ziplock bags, add a touch of water, and freeze. For lobster meat, crabmeat, and scallops, place in a plastic container or ziplock bag, cover with whole milk, and freeze.

SMOKED FISH and CORN CHOWDER for FLOYD

My friend Floyd Gelini has not eaten meat "since Memorial Day 1973" (not sure what happened that day!), but it doesn't mean he forgoes any other pleasures of the table. When I mentioned I was doing a book on chowders, we talked about this recipe concept. The salty-smoky fish in this chowder not only replaces the traditional bacon or salt pork but also provides plenty of great fish flavor. Plus it goes together very quickly and is great for a weeknight meal. Add a basket of Salt and Pepper Biscuits (page 95); an Orange, Radish, and Basil Salad (page 101); and a bowl of grapes for dessert.

4 SERVINGS

- 4 tablespoons unsalted butter
- 1 large onion, chopped
- 1 cup bottled clam juice or seafood broth (see Note)
- 2 cups water, plus more if needed
- 1 pound red-skinned potatoes, unpeeled and cut into ¾-inch dice (about 3 cups)
- 2 cups corn kernels, cut from 3 ears of corn, or frozen corn
- 2 cups heavy cream
- 8 ounces smoked peppered mackerel, smoked trout, or other smoked fish, skin and bones removed, broken into rough ¾-inch chunks
- 1½ tablespoons chopped tarragon, plus sprigs for garnish
- Freshly ground black pepper (if not using peppered fish)
- Salt, if needed

1. Melt the butter in a large heavy soup pot or Dutch oven, add the onion, and cook over medium heat until it begins to soften, about 5 minutes. Add the clam juice, water, potatoes, and corn, and bring to a boil. Reduce the heat to medium-low and cook, covered, until the potatoes are tender, about 15 minutes.

2. Add the cream, smoked fish, and tarragon, and season with pepper, if using. Bring to a simmer and cook gently for 5 minutes to blend the flavors. Add salt if needed. Let the chowder sit at cool room temperature for at least an hour before serving or, better yet, refrigerate overnight.

3. Reheat over low heat. Ladle into bowls, garnish with a tarragon sprig, and serve.

NOTE
Bottled clam juice is usually shelved with the canned fish in the supermarket; seafood broth — in cans or shelf-stable cartons, or in jars as a concentrate — can usually be found with the canned chicken and beef broth.

NOR'EASTER
BAKED FISH CHOWDER

Not all chowders need to be made on top of the stove. I came across this oven-baked version in an old Nantucket community cookbook, and I think it makes a lovely dinner-party presentation, especially on a stormy winter evening. Add Winter Greens with Apple, Walnuts, and Blue Cheese (page 107); Salt and Pepper Biscuits (page 95); and Cranberry-Apple Upside-Down Cake (page 126) for a splendid meal.

6 SERVINGS

4 ounces salt pork or bacon, cut into ½-inch dice or ground in the food processor (about 1 cup) (see Notes)

3 tablespoons butter, plus more if needed

1 large onion, thinly sliced

2 celery stalks, thinly sliced

½ cup dry white wine

1½ pounds all-purpose potatoes, peeled and thinly sliced (about 4½ cups)

¾ teaspoon salt, plus more if needed

¼ teaspoon black pepper

2 tablespoons chopped thyme

3 cups bottled clam juice or seafood broth (see Notes)

1 cup water

1½ cups heavy cream

1 large bay leaf, broken in half

2 pounds haddock, cod, or other mild flaky white fish fillets, cut into 4-inch chunks

1. Cook the salt pork with the butter in a large heavy flameproof casserole over medium-low heat until crisp and the fat is rendered, 10 to 15 minutes. Remove the cooked bits with a slotted spoon, drain on paper towels, and reserve. If you don't have 5 tablespoons of fat in the pot, make up the difference with additional butter.

2. Add the onion and celery and cook over medium heat until they begin to soften, about 5 minutes. Add the wine and boil until most of the liquid is evaporated, about 2 minutes. (You can do these steps in a skillet and scrape the vegetables into a large, deep baking dish.)

3. Preheat the oven to 400°F/200°C.

4. Layer the potatoes over the onion mixture in the baking dish and sprinkle with the salt, pepper, and thyme. Pour in the clam juice, water, and cream, and add the bay leaf. Cover (use foil if the baking dish has no lid) and bake in the preheated oven for 35 to 45 minutes, or until the potatoes are nearly tender.

5. Arrange the fish over the potatoes, gently pushing it down into the liquid. Return to the oven and bake, uncovered, until the fish is cooked through, 10 to 15 minutes. Adjust the

seasonings if necessary. The chowder can sit in the turned-off oven for up to 45 minutes, or remove the pot from the oven and let sit at cool room temperature for an hour or two.

6. Reheat the chowder if necessary in the oven at 350°F/180°C for about 15 minutes. To serve, ladle the solids into soup bowls and spoon the liquid over. Pass the reserved pork bits (reheated in the microwave) for sprinkling on the chowder if desired.

NOTES

If you're using bacon it should produce enough of its own fat, so there's no need to cook it in butter. After removing the cooked bits, you should have about 2 tablespoons of bacon fat; discard any excess and add 3 tablespoons butter to make a total of 5 table-spoons fat.

Bottled clam juice is usually shelved with the canned fish in the supermarket; seafood broth — in cans or shelf-stable cartons, or in jars as a concentrate — can usually be found with the canned chicken and beef broth.

MOBY DICK'S NANTUCKET CHOWDER

"Fishiest of all fishy places [on Nantucket] was the Try Pots, which well deserved its name; for the pots there were always boiling chowders. Chowder for breakfast, and chowder for dinner, and chowder for supper, till you began to look for fish-bones coming through your clothes."
— Herman Melville, *Moby Dick*

CLASSIC DOWN EAST
HADDOCK CHOWDER

The virtue of classic Maine-style fish chowder is its simplicity. It's a milky, brothy chowder that tastes mostly of the good, fresh, locally caught fish from which it is made. You can most certainly make this with bacon, but salt pork is traditional.

This chowder definitely benefits from the aging process (see page 5), during which all its elements have a chance to meld and blend, resulting in a most successful and happy marriage. It's great with Kale Toasts (page 96), a simple tomato or tossed green salad, and a plate of Oversize Oatmeal-Raisin Cookies (page 123) for dessert.

4–5 SERVINGS

- 4 ounces salt pork or bacon, cut into ½-inch dice or ground in the food processor (about 1 cup) (see Notes)
- 2 tablespoons butter, plus more if needed
- 1 large onion, chopped
- 2 cups bottled clam juice or seafood broth (see Notes)
- 1½ cups water
- 1 pound all-purpose potatoes, peeled and diced (about 3 cups)
- 1 cup heavy cream
- 2 tablespoons chopped fresh thyme or 2 teaspoons dried
- 1½ pounds haddock or other mild flaky white fish fillets, cut into 6-inch pieces
- Salt and freshly ground black pepper

1. Cook the salt pork with the butter in a large heavy soup pot or Dutch oven over medium-low heat until crisp and the fat is rendered, 10 to 15 minutes. Remove the cooked bits with a slotted spoon, drain on paper towels, and reserve. If you don't have 4 tablespoons of fat in the pot, make up the difference with additional butter.

2. Add the onion and cook over medium heat until it begins to soften, about 5 minutes. Add the clam juice, water, and potatoes, and bring to a boil. Reduce the heat to medium-low and cook, covered, until the potatoes are tender, about 15 minutes.

3. Add the cream and thyme, then add the fish, and cook, uncovered, over low heat until the fish is opaque, about 3 minutes. The fish will break apart as it cooks and is gently stirred. Season with salt and pepper to taste. Let the chowder sit at cool room temperature for at least an hour or, better yet, refrigerate overnight.

4. Reheat over very low heat, ladle into bowls, and pass the reserved pork bits (reheated in the microwave) for sprinkling on the chowder if desired.

NOTES

If you're using bacon it should produce enough of its own fat, so there's no need to cook it in butter. After removing the cooked bits, you should have about 2 tablespoons of bacon fat; discard any excess and add 2 tablespoons butter to make a total of 4 tablespoons fat.

Bottled clam juice is usually shelved with the canned fish in the supermarket; seafood broth — in cans or shelf-stable cartons, or in jars as a concentrate — can usually be found with the canned chicken and beef broth.

CHOWDER AND MARCHING SOCIETIES

It is thought that chowder and marching societies were originally organized during pre-Revolutionary times when groups of citizens gathered together over chowder to discuss current affairs and then march into town to air their grievances. "Chowder and marching societies" has in recent times become the arch name given to groups around the country that meet to promote civic welfare with festive gatherings. A Google search turns up many such clubs nationwide.

BERMUDA FISH CHOWDER

- 8 ounces bacon, cut into ½-inch pieces (about 2 cups)
- 4 tablespoons olive oil
- 2 large onions, chopped
- 4 celery stalks, chopped
- 1 green bell pepper, seeded and chopped
- 3 garlic cloves, finely chopped
- 8 cups water, plus additional as the chowder cooks
- 3 pounds firm white fish such as haddock, cod, grouper, tilefish, or snapper, cut into 4-inch chunks
- 1 (28-ounce) can diced tomatoes with juice
- 1 (32-ounce) carton shelf-stable beef broth
- 2 pounds all-purpose potatoes, peeled and diced (about 6 cups)
- 3 carrots, diced
- 3 bay leaves
- ½ cup dark rum, preferably Gosling's Black Seal, plus additional for the table
- 3 tablespoons Sherry Peppers Sauce, plus additional for the table (see Note)
- 1½ teaspoons salt, plus more if needed
- 3 tablespoons Worcestershire sauce
- 2 tablespoons dried thyme
- 1 teaspoon ground cloves
- 1 teaspoon curry powder
- Freshly ground black pepper
- Juice of 1 lemon
- 3 tablespoons chopped flat-leaf parsley

I never knew my Bermudian grandmother, but she was reputed to be a wonderful cook. Needless to say, Bermuda fish chowder — the island's national dish — was one of her specialties. Her recipe was passed down to my aunt Mary Gordon, who made it for us a few times, with memorable results.

The cooking method runs counter to all other chowders, demanding hours-long simmering and stirring, which results in an alchemic melding of the disparate ingredients into a dark and mysteriously potent brew. Bermuda-bottled Outerbridge's Sherry Peppers — a piquant sauce of secret herbs, spices, and chile peppers — is a key ingredient, as is the dark rum. Follow it up with Sour Lemon Tart in a Graham Cracker Crust (page 121).

8 SERVINGS

1. Cook the bacon with the oil in a very large heavy soup pot or Dutch oven over medium-low heat until crisp and the fat is rendered, 10 to 15 minutes. Leave the bacon and drippings in the pot.

2. Add the onions, celery, bell pepper, and garlic, and cook over medium heat until the vegetables begin to soften and brown lightly, about 8 minutes. Add the water, fish, tomatoes, beef broth, potatoes, carrots, bay leaves, rum, pepper sauce, salt, Worcestershire, thyme, cloves, and curry powder. Bring to a boil, then reduce the heat to low and cook, uncovered, for 3 hours, stirring quite frequently to prevent scorching. Keep adding more water if the chowder reduces and thickens too much. The fish and potatoes will break down and the

chowder will develop a rich, dark color and fairly thick texture. Season with pepper and additional salt if needed.

3. Unlike most chowders, this one does not need to age. Serve immediately, set aside at cool room temperature for an hour or so, or refrigerate for up to 2 days. This chowder also freezes well.

4. When ready to serve, reheat if necessary over low heat. Stir in the lemon juice and parsley, ladle into bowls, and pass pitchers of rum and pepper sauce at the table.

NOTE
Sherry Peppers Sauce can be ordered from the Outerbridge website (www.outerbridge.com). If you can't get it, use Madeira or a semi-sweet sherry and add ½ teaspoon or so of liquid hot pepper sauce.

CHOWDER PARTIES
From about the mid-1800s, chowder parties became a popular summer pastime on the New England coast. Families would pack up ingredients for chowder along with other food such as bread, cheese, and pies to round out the meal and head to the beach for a party, with chowder making as the primary amusement. An iron kettle was set up on a tripod over a driftwood fire, and the chowder (sometimes using fish caught from the shore) simmered while people relaxed, fished, sailed, and played games. An experienced cook called the chowder master oversaw the proceedings.

NORTHWEST SALMON CHOWDER with LEEKS and PEAS

4 ounces bacon, cut into ½-inch pieces (about 1 cup)

2 tablespoons butter, plus more if needed

1 medium onion, chopped

1 large leek, cleaned, cut in half lengthwise, and thinly sliced (white and pale green parts only)

1 cup bottled clam juice or seafood broth (see Notes)

½ cup dry white wine

2 cups water

1 pound red-skinned potatoes, unpeeled and diced (about 3 cups)

¾ teaspoon salt, plus more if needed

1 cup heavy cream

1¼ pounds salmon, skin and any bones removed, cut into 3-inch chunks

1 cup fresh or frozen peas (see Notes)

½ cup snipped chives or thinly sliced scallions

2 tablespoons coarsely chopped dill, plus sprigs for garnish

Freshly ground black pepper

Is there a prettier or more delicious fish than salmon? There's plenty of it in the Northwest, and this chowder showcases its gorgeous color and is enhanced by red-skinned potatoes, leeks, peas, and dill. Serve it with Beet Salad on Arugula with Ricotta Salata (page 99), Red Pepper–Scallion Pita Toasts (page 91), and a fruit dessert such as Plum-Almond Galette (page 117).

4 SERVINGS

1. Cook the bacon in a large heavy soup pot or Dutch oven over medium-low heat until crisp and the fat is rendered, 10 to 15 minutes. Remove the cooked bits with a slotted spoon, drain on paper towels, and reserve. You should have 2 tablespoons of fat in the pot; if there is too much, pour some off, or if there is too little, make up the difference with additional butter.

2. Add the butter to the pot and cook the onion and leek over medium heat until they begin to soften, about 5 minutes. Add the clam juice, wine, water, potatoes, and salt, and bring to a boil. Reduce the heat to medium-low and cook, uncovered, until the potatoes are almost tender, about 12 minutes.

3. Add the cream and salmon and bring to a simmer over medium heat. Cook, uncovered, until the fish is opaque, about 5 minutes. The fish will break apart as it cooks. ⊖

4. Add the peas, chives, and dill, and cook for 5 minutes if using fresh peas or about 2 minutes for frozen peas. Stir in the reserved bacon bits and season with pepper and additional salt if needed. Let the chowder sit at cool room temperature for at least an hour, or refrigerate overnight.

5. Reheat over very low heat. Use a slotted spoon to ladle salmon, potatoes, and peas into shallow bowls, then ladle the broth over the top. Garnish with dill sprigs and serve.

NOTES

Bottled clam juice is usually shelved with the canned fish in the supermarket; seafood broth — in cans or shelf-stable cartons, or in jars as a concentrate — can usually be found with the canned chicken and beef broth.

If making the chowder a day ahead, add the peas and herbs when reheating, since they will lose color upon standing.

DANIEL WEBSTER'S FISH CHOWDER RECIPE

"Take a cod of ten pounds, well cleaned, leaving on the skin. Cut into pieces one and a half pounds thick, preserving the head whole. Take one and a half pounds of clear, fat salt pork, cut in thin slices. Do the same with twelve potatoes. Take the largest pot you have. Try out the pork first, then take out the pieces of pork, leaving in the drippings. Add to that three parts of water, a layer of fish, so as to cover the bottom of the pot; next a layer of potatoes, then two tablespoons of salt, 1 teaspoon of pepper, then the pork, another layer of fish, and the remainder of the potatoes.

"Fill the pot with water to cover the ingredients. Put over a good fire. Let the chowder boil twenty-five minutes. When this is done have a quart of boiling milk ready, and ten hard crackers split and dipped in cold water. Add milk and crackers. Let the whole boil five minutes. The chowder is then ready to be first-rate if you have followed the directions. An onion may be added if you like the flavor.

"This chowder is suitable for a large fishing party."

From *The New England Yankee Cook Book*, edited by Imogene Wolcott

LOBSTER and SWEET CORN CHOWDER

7 cups water

1 teaspoon salt, plus more if needed

4 live lobsters (1¼ to 1½ pounds each), rinsed (see Note)

6 ounces bacon, cut into ½-inch pieces (about 1½ cups)

5 tablespoons butter, plus more if needed

1 large onion, chopped

1 large celery stalk, thinly sliced

3 tablespoons all-purpose flour

½ cup dry white wine

1 pound all-purpose potatoes, peeled and diced (about 3 cups)

2 cups corn kernels, cut from 3 ears of corn, or frozen corn

2 tablespoons chopped thyme

2 cups heavy cream

¼ teaspoon cayenne pepper

Freshly ground black pepper

This is an utterly scrumptious and beautiful chowder. With chunks of pink lobster meat, nuggets of yellow corn, flecks of thyme, and pools of melted butter, it makes a stellar summer dinner-party main course. This special chowder is especially good accompanied by Kale Toasts (page 96). Lattice-Top Blueberry Pie (page 114) is the ideal finish.

6 SERVINGS

1. Bring the water to a boil in a large soup pot and add the salt. Add the lobsters, cover, and return to a boil. Cook, covered, over medium-low heat until the lobsters are bright red and fully cooked, 14 to 17 minutes. (Hard-shell lobsters will take the longer cooking time.) Use tongs to remove the lobsters to a bowl, leaving the cooking liquid in the pot.

2. Remove the claws and tails and set aside, rinse off most of the tomalley (green material) from the lobster bodies, and return three of the bodies to the pot. (Discard the fourth body.) Return to a boil, reduce the heat to low, and cook for 15 minutes. Strain through a medium-mesh strainer into a bowl. Measure out 5 cups of the broth, which will be tinted a pretty pale green from the lobster bodies. Meanwhile, pick out the lobster claw and tail meat, chop into bite-size pieces, and refrigerate. (This can be done up to 24 hours ahead.)

3. Cook the bacon in a large heavy soup pot or Dutch oven over medium-low heat until crisp and the fat is rendered, 10 to 15 minutes. Remove the cooked bits with a slotted spoon, →

drain on paper towels, and reserve. You should have 3 table-spoons of fat in the pot; if there is too much, pour some off, or if there is too little, make up the difference with additional butter.

4. Add the butter to the pot and cook the onion and celery over medium heat until they begin to soften, about 5 minutes. Add the flour and cook, stirring, for 1 minute.

5. Add the wine, raise the heat to high, and boil briskly until the liquid is reduced by about half, about 4 minutes. Add the reserved lobster broth, potatoes, corn, and thyme, and return to a boil. Reduce the heat to low and cook, covered, until the potatoes are tender, about 15 minutes.

6. Add the reserved lobster meat, cream, and cayenne, and cook, uncovered, for 5 minutes. Stir in the reserved bacon bits and season with pepper and additional salt if needed. Let the chowder sit at cool room temperature for at least an hour or, better yet, refrigerate overnight.

7. Reheat over low heat, adding more broth, milk, or water if the chowder is too thick. Ladle into bowls and serve.

NOTE

You can also use 1 pound of chopped picked-out lobster meat and 5 cups of seafood broth, clam juice, or a combination of clam juice and water. Seafood broth — in cans or shelf-stable cartons, or in jars as a concentrate — can usually be found with the canned chicken and beef broth in the supermarket; bottled clam juice is usually shelved with the canned fish.

STONINGTON MIXED SEAFOOD CHOWDER

2 pounds medium-size soft-shell clams (25 to 30 clams) (see Note)

3 cups water

½ cup (1 stick) butter

1 large onion, chopped

1½ pounds all-purpose potatoes, peeled and diced (about 4½ cups)

1½ pounds haddock or other mild flaky fish fillets, cut into large chunks

8 ounces shelled small shrimp

8 ounces sea scallops, cut in halves or thirds longitudinally

2 (12-ounce) cans evaporated milk

Salt and freshly ground black pepper

¼ cup chopped flat-leaf parsley

Fisherman's Friend Restaurant in Stonington, Maine, has served a mixed seafood chowder made with local fish for upward of 30 years now. Wheedle as I might, they are reluctant to part with their recipe, so I've analyzed it (meaning I've eaten bowls of the chowder every chance I get) and tinkered with a formula that is pretty darn close, I think.

Vinegary Cabbage Slaw (page 105) is an ideal accompaniment, along with oyster crackers or French bread. Dark and Sticky Candied Gingerbread (page 129) would complete the meal beautifully.

4–6 SERVINGS

1. Scrub the clams well and rinse in several changes of water if they are muddy. (See About Clams, page 13.) Bring the water to a boil in a large pot, add the clams, and return to a boil. Reduce the heat to medium-low and cook, covered, shaking the pot a couple of times to redistribute the clams, until they open, about 5 minutes. Use a slotted spoon to transfer the clams to a bowl. Pour the clam broth into another bowl, leaving any sediment behind.

2. Working over the bowl to catch juices, remove the clams from their shells. Pull off the black skin and snip off the black necks if you don't like the looks of them in your chowder. ⤳

Cut the clams with a large knife or scissors into approximately ¾-inch pieces and set them aside. Let the broth stand for at least 30 minutes, then measure out 3 cups, leaving any additional black sediment behind. (Clams and broth can be prepared a day ahead. Cover and refrigerate.)

3. Melt the butter in a large heavy soup pot or Dutch oven over medium heat. Add the onion and cook until it begins to soften, about 5 minutes. Add the 3 cups broth and the potatoes and bring to a boil. Reduce the heat to medium-low and cook, covered, until the potatoes are almost tender, about 13 minutes.

4. Add the haddock, shrimp, and scallops, and cook until the seafood is cooked through, 3 to 5 minutes. Add the cooked clams and the evaporated milk and bring just to a simmer. Season with salt and pepper to taste. Let the chowder sit at cool room temperature for at least an hour or, better yet, refrigerate overnight.

5. Reheat over low heat and stir in the parsley. Ladle into bowls and serve.

NOTE

Or use a 10-ounce can of whole baby clams, supplementing the juice in the can with 3 cups bottled clam juice or seafood broth. Bottled clam juice is usually shelved with the canned fish in the supermarket; seafood broth — in cans or shelf-stable cartons, or in jars as a concentrate — can usually be found with the canned chicken and beef broth.

THE DUMBING DOWN OF CHOWDER

Some credit (or discredit) chain restaurateur Howard Johnson for foisting his commercial version of overly thickened, whiter-than-white, flavorless clam chowder on an unsuspecting public, thereby lowering chowder standards nationwide.

MUSSEL CHOWDER
with LIGHT CURRY
and COLORFUL VEGETABLES

3 pounds mussels

4 cups water

2 cups dry white wine

5 tablespoons butter

2 tablespoons olive oil

1¼ pounds all-purpose potatoes, peeled and diced
(about 3¾ cups)

¾ teaspoon salt, plus more
if needed

2 carrots, thinly sliced

1 leek, cleaned, cut in half
lengthwise, and thinly
sliced (white and pale
green parts only)

1 yellow bell pepper,
seeded and chopped

1 large shallot, chopped

2 garlic cloves, finely
chopped

1 teaspoon curry powder

1 cup heavy cream

Freshly ground black pepper

2 tablespoons chopped flat-
leaf parsley

Mussels are great in so many ways. They are plentiful, inexpensive, beautiful, and delicious — plus these days, since most are farm raised, they don't need much scrubbing or debearding. I also love making chowders with whole, intact bivalves, if possible, because they make such a lovely broth.

This lightly curried brew is meat-free and is flecked with carrot, leek, and yellow bell pepper, making for a chowder that is beautiful to behold. Brussels Sprout Slaw (page 100) is a good go-with, along with Crusty Skillet Cornbread (page 89), and perhaps Strawberry-Rhubarb Cobbler (page 124) or Plum-Almond Galette (page 117) to complete the meal.

4–6 SERVINGS

1. Scrub the mussels and debeard if necessary. (See About Mussels, page 46.) Combine the mussels, water, and wine in a large pot and bring to a boil. Reduce the heat to medium-low and cook, covered, shaking the pot to redistribute the mussels, until they open, 4 to 6 minutes depending on size. Use a slotted spoon to transfer the mussels to a bowl, discarding any that do not open.

2. Set aside 16 mussels in their shells and shuck the rest. Pour the mussel broth into a bowl, leaving any sediment behind,  →

and set aside for at least 30 minutes, then measure out 4 cups, leaving any additional sediment behind. The broth will be a steel-gray color. Add water if necessary to make 4 cups. (Mussels and broth can be prepared a day ahead. Cover and refrigerate.)

3. Heat the butter and oil in a large heavy soup pot or Dutch oven. Add the potatoes and salt and cook over medium heat, stirring occasionally, for 5 minutes. Add the carrots, leek, bell pepper, and shallot, and cook, covered, over low heat until all the vegetables are almost tender, about 12 minutes. Add the garlic and curry powder and cook, stirring, for 1 minute.

4. Add the reserved mussel broth, leaving any lingering sediment behind. Bring to a simmer and cook until the potatoes are fully tender, about 5 minutes. Add the cream and the shucked mussels and cook gently for 3 minutes to blend the flavors. Season with pepper and additional salt if needed. Let sit at cool room temperature for at least an hour or, better yet, refrigerate overnight.

5. When ready to serve, add the reserved mussels in their shells and reheat over low heat. Ladle into bowls, making sure that each serving contains at least 2 mussels in their shells. Sprinkle with the parsley and serve.

ABOUT MUSSELS

Most mussels are farm raised these days and need only a quick rinse before cooking. If you have wild mussels, scrub them with a stiff brush and use your fingers or a knife to pull off the wiry beards. If they're muddy, let them soak in a couple of bowls of cold salted water for about an hour, lifting them from one bowl to the other, changing and swishing the water and repeating the process until the water is almost clear of any sediment.

STORING

Mussels can live out of salt water in the refrigerator for several days. Store them in the lowest part of the refrigerator on ice. They cannot sit in melted ice water, so drain off water if necessary. Store in mesh bags or plastic bags with holes. If kept in airtight plastic they will suffocate.

ALIVE?

Check to make sure mussels are alive before cooking. Dead mussels will gape open and won't respond if you knock their shells together or try to squeeze them closed. If they close up somewhat they're alive; any that don't react at all should be tossed.

SHRIMP, FENNEL, and RED POTATO CHOWDER

½ cup (1 stick) butter

2 medium onions, chopped

½ teaspoon fennel seeds, crushed or finely chopped

3 tablespoons all-purpose flour

5 cups shrimp broth, bottled clam juice, or seafood broth (see Notes)

1 cup water

2 cups half-and-half

1½ pounds red-skinned potatoes, unpeeled, halved or quartered and sliced (about 4½ cups)

1 fennel bulb (about 8 ounces), halved and thinly sliced, plus 3 tablespoons chopped fennel fronds for garnish

¾ teaspoon salt, plus more if needed

2 pounds unshelled shrimp — either small Maine shrimp or any small or medium-size shrimp — or 1½ pounds shelled and deveined shrimp

1 teaspoon smoked paprika

Freshly ground black pepper

3 tablespoons Pernod (optional; see Notes)

¼ cup snipped chives

This pretty pink and white chowder can be made with any shrimp of almost any size, but if you get the extra-large or jumbo size, cut them into slightly smaller pieces. Use fresh or thawed frozen shrimp in the shells (which you will have to peel and devein) or frozen shelled shrimp — either cooked or uncooked. This meat-free chowder is great with Winter Greens with Apple, Walnuts, and Blue Cheese (page 107); Salt and Pepper Biscuits (page 95); and Lemon Sponge Pudding Cake (page 113) for dessert.

6 SERVINGS

1. Melt the butter in a large heavy soup pot or Dutch oven and cook the onions over medium heat until they begin to soften, about 5 minutes. Add the fennel seeds and cook for 1 minute.

2. Add the flour, whisk for 2 minutes, then whisk in the broth, water, and half-and-half. Add the potatoes, fennel, and salt, and bring to a boil. Reduce the heat to medium-low and cook, covered, until the potatoes are tender, about 15 minutes.

3. If the shrimp are unshelled, peel and devein. Add the shrimp and paprika, bring just to a simmer, and remove from the heat. Season with pepper and additional salt if needed. Let the chowder sit at cool room temperature for at least an hour or, better yet, refrigerate overnight. ⊙→

4. Reheat over low heat, adding more broth, milk, or water if the chowder is too thick. Stir in the Pernod, if using, and chives. Ladle into bowls, sprinkle with fennel fronds, and serve.

NOTES

To make a quick broth from the shrimp shells, combine the shells in a pot with 1 teaspoon salt and 5 cups water. Bring to a boil, then reduce the heat to low and cook, covered, for 20 minutes. Strain. Or you can use bottled clam juice or canned seafood broth, or a combination of any of the above.

Pernod is an anise-flavored liqueur; use it if you like a stronger anise flavor.

NORA EPHRON ON COOKING

"What I love about cooking is that after a hard day, there is something comforting about the fact that if you melt butter and add flour and then hot stock, it will get thick! It's a sure thing!"

FENNEL

DOUBLE CORN
SUMMER CHOWDER

A surprising amount of corn flavor is released when the cobs are simmered in water, which helps amplify the corniness of this lovely summer chowder. It's great with Grilled Summer Vegetable Salad with Balsamic Drizzle (page 104) and Rosemary-Onion Focaccia (page 93) or plain toasted focaccia.

4 SERVINGS

- 6 ears corn
- 5 cups water
- 1 teaspoon salt, plus more if needed
- 4 ounces bacon, cut into ½-inch pieces (about 1 cup)
- 2 tablespoons butter, plus more if needed
- 1 large onion, chopped
- 2 tablespoons all-purpose flour
- 2 cups half-and-half
- 12 ounces all-purpose potatoes, peeled and diced (about 2¼ cups)
- 3 tablespoons chopped fresh thyme
- 1 teaspoon sugar
- Freshly ground black pepper

CORN OR SEX?

"People have tried and they have tried, but sex is not better than sweet corn."
— Garrison Keillor

1. Cut the kernels off the corn and reserve them. (You should have 4 to 5 cups.) Place the corncobs in a large pot, cover with the water, add the salt, and bring to a boil. Reduce the heat to low and cook, covered, for 30 minutes. Leave the cobs in the broth until ready to use.

2. Cook the bacon in a large heavy soup pot or Dutch oven over medium-low heat until crisp and the fat is rendered, 10 to 15 minutes. Remove the cooked bits with a slotted spoon, drain on paper towels, and reserve. You should have 2 tablespoons of fat in the pot; if there is too much, pour some off, or if there is too little, make up the difference with additional butter.

3. Add the butter to the pot and cook the onion over medium heat until it begins to soften, about 5 minutes. Add the flour and whisk until thick and bubbly, about 3 minutes. Measure out 4 cups of the corn broth and add to the pot along with the half-and-half. Whisk over medium-high heat until the mixture comes to a simmer.

4. Add the reserved corn kernels, potatoes, thyme, and sugar, and cook, covered, over medium-low heat until the corn and potatoes are tender, about 15 minutes. Stir in the reserved bacon bits and season with pepper and additional salt if needed. Let the chowder sit at cool room temperature for at least an hour or, better yet, refrigerate overnight.

5. Reheat over low heat, ladle into bowls, and serve.

VINEYARD CHICKEN and CORN CHOWDER

One thinks of the typical chowder as being made with seafood, but in fact, New Englanders often use other ingredients, including chicken parts. I first made this chowder one stormy day on Martha's Vineyard and now make it often for weeknight suppers. A salad such as Winter Greens with Apple, Walnuts, and Blue Cheese (page 107) is a great side dish. Pass a plate of Black Pepper Brownies (page 119) to complete the meal.

4–6 SERVINGS

4 ounces bacon, cut into ½-inch pieces (about 1 cup)

1 large onion, chopped

3 celery stalks, thinly sliced

4 cups water

1½ pounds skin-on chicken thighs

1 teaspoon salt, plus more if needed

1½ pounds all-purpose potatoes, partially peeled and diced (about 4½ cups)

3 cups frozen corn (see Note)

2 cups half-and-half

2 tablespoons chopped fresh sage or 2 teaspoons dried

Freshly ground black pepper

1. Cook the bacon in a large heavy soup pot or Dutch oven over medium-low heat until crisp and the fat is rendered, 10 to 15 minutes. Remove the cooked bits with a slotted spoon, drain on paper towels, and reserve, leaving the drippings in the pot.

2. Add the onion and celery to the pot and cook over medium heat until they begin to soften, about 5 minutes. Add the water, chicken, and salt, and bring to a boil. Reduce the heat to low and cook, covered, until the chicken is tender, about 30 minutes. Remove the chicken to a bowl and set aside.

3. Add the potatoes to the pot and cook, covered, over medium heat until tender, about 15 minutes. Meanwhile, when the chicken is cool enough to handle, strip the meat off the bones and shred or cut it into bite-size pieces. Discard the skin and bones. If much fat is visible on the broth, skim some off and discard.

4. Add the corn, half-and-half, sage, and shredded chicken to the pot. Bring just to a simmer, stir in the reserved bacon bits, and season with pepper and additional salt if needed. This

chowder does not need aging; serve immediately or refrigerate for up to 2 days. It also freezes quite well.

5. If reheating, warm over very low heat so the chowder does not curdle. Ladle into bowls and serve.

NOTE
Since this is more of a cold-weather chowder, I usually use frozen corn, but if you have fresh corn, strip the kernels from about 4 ears and add it with the potatoes.

> **VINEYARD WISDOM**
> "Chowder, if built with due respect for both clock and calendar, improves with age. In many chowder recipes one encounters the phrase 'remove to back of stove,' and there is a good deal of eloquence there. On the back of the stove is where much of the perfection comes in."
> — *Vineyard Gazette*

SAINT PATRICK'S CHOWDER

Here is corned beef and cabbage ("boiled dinner" in New England) in a bowl. Since it has all the chowder elements — salted or cured meat, potatoes, onions, and broth — I believe it can legitimately be labeled as such. You can make it from scratch or substitute cooked leftover Saint Patrick's Day potatoes, carrots, and cabbage (see Note). Serve with a simple green salad, buttered rye toast, and Spiced Hermit Bar Cookies (page 131) to finish.

5–6 SERVINGS

- 6 tablespoons butter
- 1 large onion, chopped
- 6 cups low-sodium chicken broth (see Note)
- 2 cups water, plus more if needed
- 1½ pounds red-skinned potatoes, unpeeled and diced (about 4½ cups)
- 5 carrots, sliced
- 2 tablespoons chopped fresh thyme or 2 teaspoons dried
- 1 pound cooked corned beef, shredded into bite-size pieces or cut into ½-inch dice (about 4 cups)
- 10 ounces cabbage, sliced (about 4 cups)
- 2 tablespoons whole-grain mustard
- Freshly ground black pepper
- Salt, if needed
- 3 tablespoons chopped flat-leaf parsley

1. Melt the butter in a large soup pot. Add the onion and cook over medium heat until it begins to soften, about 5 minutes. Add the broth and water, along with the potatoes, carrots, and thyme. Bring to a boil, then reduce the heat to low and cook, covered, for 10 minutes.

2. Add the corned beef and cabbage and cook, uncovered, over medium heat until the potatoes and cabbage are tender, about 10 minutes. Whisk in the mustard and season with pepper to taste; it may not need salt due to the saltiness of the corned beef. This chowder does not necessarily need aging. Serve immediately, let it sit at room temperature for an hour or two, or cool and refrigerate for up to 2 days.

3. If reheating, warm over low heat, adding a bit more water if needed. Stir in the parsley, ladle into bowls, and serve.

NOTE

Corned beef cooking water can substitute for some or all of the broth if it is not too salty. If you have leftover potatoes, carrots, or cabbage, add them with the corned beef and cook for only 5 minutes.

DAY-after-THANKSGIVING CHOWDER

This truly scrumptious chowder is an ideal use for leftovers from the Thanksgiving meal, or of course you can make it any time of the year. Beet Salad on Arugula with Ricotta Salata (page 99) is a great side dish, along with some leftover Thanksgiving rolls. If you're feeling ambitious, Cranberry-Apple Upside-Down Cake (page 126) is the ideal dessert.

5–6 SERVINGS

4 ounces bacon, cut into ½-inch pieces (about 1 cup)

2 tablespoons butter, plus more if needed

1 large onion, chopped

1 large celery stalk, thinly sliced

4 cups turkey broth or 1 (32-ounce) carton shelf-stable chicken broth (see Notes)

1½ pounds all-purpose potatoes, peeled and diced (about 4½ cups)

2 tablespoons chopped sage

1 tablespoon poultry seasoning mix (see Notes)

½ teaspoon salt, plus more if needed

3 cups shredded or diced turkey meat

2 cups half-and-half

2 cups cooked vegetables, such as carrots, peas, green beans, or Brussels sprouts, diced if necessary (see Notes)

Freshly ground black pepper

1. Cook the bacon in a large heavy soup pot or Dutch oven over medium-low heat until crisp and the fat is rendered, 10 to 15 minutes. Remove the cooked bits with a slotted spoon, drain on paper towels, and reserve. You should have 2 tablespoons of fat in the pot; if there is too much, pour some off, or if there is too little, make up the difference with additional butter.

2. Add the butter to the pot and cook the onion and celery over medium heat until they begin to soften, about 5 minutes. Add the broth, potatoes, sage, poultry seasoning, and salt, and bring to a boil. Reduce the heat to medium-low and cook, covered, over medium-low heat until the potatoes are tender, about 15 minutes.

3. Add the turkey, half-and-half, and vegetables, and cook over very low heat for 2 minutes to blend the flavors. Stir in the reserved bacon and season with pepper and additional salt if needed. This chowder does not necessarily need aging; serve immediately or cool and refrigerate for up to 2 days.

4. If reheating, warm over very low heat so the chowder does not curdle. Ladle into bowls and serve.

NOTES

If you have the turkey carcass, break it up somewhat and place in a large pot. Cover with water, add an onion, a celery stalk, and

1 teaspoon salt, and cook, uncovered, for about an hour. Strain and use as the broth in this recipe. The rest of the broth can be frozen for another use.

Use a good brand of poultry seasoning blend, which includes several herbs; New Englanders are partial to Bell's Seasoning.

If you don't have leftover vegetables, cook 2 to 3 chopped carrots with the potatoes and add other more tender vegetables (fresh or frozen) toward the end of the cooking time.

REASSURING SOUP

"Chowder breathes reassurance. It steams consolation."
— Clementine Paddleford

"CALDO VERDE" CHOWDER

This classic Portuguese brew made with kale, potatoes, onions, and smoked meat is usually called a soup (it means "green broth" in Portuguese), but it's actually so akin to a chowder that I've gone ahead and included it in this chapter. If you can find linguica — the garlicky, peppery Portuguese sausage — it's a good choice because its flavors spice up the stew beautifully, but any well-seasoned cooked sausage such as kielbasa will do. Orange, Radish, and Basil Salad (page 101) complements nicely.

4 SERVINGS

- 3 tablespoons olive oil
- 6 ounces linguica, thinly sliced (about 1½ cups)
- 1 large onion, thinly sliced
- 1 (32-ounce) carton shelf-stable chicken broth
- 2 cups water, plus more if needed
- 1½ pounds all-purpose potatoes, halved and thinly sliced (about 4½ cups)
- 6 ounces kale (any type), thinly sliced crosswise (about 5 cups)
- Freshly ground black pepper

1. Heat the oil in a large soup pot or Dutch oven. Add the sausage and cook over medium heat, stirring frequently, until golden brown, about 6 minutes. Remove with a slotted spoon and reserve, leaving the drippings in the pot.

2. Add the onion and cook over medium heat until it begins to soften and brown, about 7 minutes. Add the broth, water, and potatoes, and bring to a boil. Reduce the heat to low and cook, covered, for 10 minutes.

3. Add the kale and reserved sausage and return to a boil. Reduce the heat to low and cook, covered, until the potatoes are very tender and beginning to fall apart, about 15 minutes. Thin with a bit more water if needed and season with pepper to taste; it should not need salt because the sausage is quite salty. This chowder does not need aging; serve immediately or refrigerate for up to 2 days.

4. If reheating, warm over low heat. Ladle into bowls and serve.

LATE SUMMER
SQUASH CHOWDER

- 4 ounces bacon, cut into ½-inch pieces (about 1 cup)
- 2 tablespoons butter, plus more if needed
- 1 large onion, sliced
- 1 red, green, or yellow Italian frying pepper, chopped
- 2 tablespoons all-purpose flour
- 1 (32-ounce) carton shelf-stable chicken broth
- 2 cups half-and-half
- 1 pound red- or yellow-skinned potatoes, unpeeled, halved, and sliced (about 3 cups)
- ½ teaspoon salt, plus more if needed
- 1 pound summer squash (any type), cut into ½- to ¾-inch slices or chunks (about 3 cups)
- 1½ tablespoons chopped fresh thyme
- 1½ tablespoons chopped fresh tarragon
- 1 cup shredded cheddar cheese
- Freshly ground black pepper
- Liquid hot pepper sauce

When your garden or farmers' market over-floweth with summer squash — whether it be yellow crookneck or green or yellow zucchini or pattypan — make a pot of this quick, scrumptious chowder. Also included in this brew are late-summer long skinny peppers, known as Italian frying or Cubanelle, and thin-skinned new potatoes. A handful of cheese enriches and adds pretty color. This chowder is lovely with Shingled Tomato and Nectarine Salad with Olive Vinaigrette (page 103) and toasted Rosemary-Onion Focaccia (page 93).

4 SERVINGS

1. Cook the bacon in a large heavy soup pot or Dutch oven over medium-low heat until crisp and the fat is rendered, 10 to 15 minutes. Remove the cooked bits with a slotted spoon, drain on paper towels, and reserve. You should have about 2 table-spoons of fat in the pot; if there is too much, pour some off, or if there is too little, make up the difference with additional butter.

2. Add the butter to the pot and cook the onion over medium heat until it begins to soften, about 5 minutes. Add the frying pepper and cook for 1 minute. Add the flour and whisk until thick and bubbly, about 2 minutes.

3. Add the broth and half-and-half and whisk over high heat until the mixture comes to a simmer. Add the potatoes and salt and cook, covered, over medium-low heat for 5 minutes.

4. Add the squash, thyme, and tarragon, and continue cooking until the potatoes and squash are both very tender, 10 to 15 minutes. Remove the pot from the heat and stir in the cheese. Stir in the reserved bacon bits and season with pepper and additional salt if needed. Let the chowder sit at cool room temperature for at least an hour or, better yet, refrigerate overnight.

5. Reheat over low heat and ladle into bowls. Pass the hot sauce at the table.

> ### JUDITH JONES ON COOKING
> "Cooking demands attention, patience, and, above all, a respect for the gifts of the earth. It is a form of worship, a way of giving thanks."

SUCCOTASH CHOWDER
with TOMATOES and BASIL

Succotash, a Native American dish made up of stewed beans and corn, was a welcome addition to the early New England table, and the combination later found its way into inland chowders. I found a version of succotash chowder in an old New England cookbook, its headnote claiming that the recipe could be traced back more than 250 years in one Maine family. It's still good today, especially with the addition of a bit of fresh tomato and basil to enliven the brew. A pan of Crusty Skillet Cornbread (page 89) would be a nice addition for a simple supper.

4 SERVINGS

4 ounces bacon, cut into ½-inch pieces (about 1 cup)

1 large onion, chopped

1 teaspoon dry mustard

1 (32-ounce) carton shelf-stable chicken broth

1 pound red-skinned potatoes, unpeeled and diced (about 3 cups)

3 cups corn kernels, cut from about 4 ears of corn, or frozen corn

1 (10-ounce) package frozen baby lima beans (about 2½ cups)

1 teaspoon sugar

¾ teaspoon salt, plus more if needed

1 cup seeded and diced fresh ripe tomatoes (or drained canned diced tomatoes)

2 cups half-and-half

3 tablespoons slivered fresh basil

Freshly ground black pepper

1. Cook the bacon in a large heavy soup pot or Dutch oven over medium-low heat until crisp and the fat is rendered, 10 to 15 minutes. Add the onion and cook over medium heat until it begins to soften, about 5 minutes. Add the mustard and cook, stirring, for 1 minute.

2. Add the broth, potatoes, corn, beans, sugar, and salt, and bring to a boil. Reduce the heat to low and cook, covered, until the potatoes and other vegetables are tender, about 15 minutes. Add the tomatoes and cook, uncovered, for about 5 minutes.

3. Stir in the half-and-half and basil and cook over very low heat for 2 minutes to blend the flavors. Season with pepper and additional salt if needed. Let the chowder sit at cool room temperature for at least an hour or, better yet, refrigerate overnight.

4. Reheat over very low heat so the chowder does not curdle. Ladle into bowls and serve.

SPRING-DUG PARSNIP CHOWDER

4 ounces salt pork or bacon, cut into ½-inch dice or ground in the food processor (about 1 cup) (see Note)

2 tablespoons butter, plus more if needed

1 large onion, chopped

1 (14½-ounce) can chicken broth

1½ pounds parsnips, peeled and cut into ¼-inch-thick slices (about 4½ cups)

1 pound all-purpose potatoes, peeled and sliced or diced (about 3 cups)

¾ teaspoon salt, plus more if needed

About 1 cup water

2 cups half-and-half

Freshly ground black pepper

3 tablespoons chopped flat-leaf parsley or snipped chives

This farmhouse chowder, especially popular in Vermont (and sometimes called a stew there), is a homely brew, cooked in the late winter in the old days as a way to stretch vegetables from the root cellar. Now parsnips — particularly the extra-sweet "spring dug" variety — have come into their own and are proudly featured in farmers' markets and served at white-tablecloth restaurants. I prefer salt pork here because smoky bacon tends to overwhelm the subtle sweet spiciness of the parsnips. Baby Kale Salad with Pine Nuts (page 108) would be a wonderful accompaniment.

4 SERVINGS

1. Cook the salt pork with the butter in a large heavy soup pot or Dutch oven over medium-low heat until crisp and the fat is rendered, 10 to 15 minutes. Remove the cooked bits with a slotted spoon, drain on paper towels, and reserve. If you don't have 4 tablespoons of fat in the pot, make up the difference with additional butter.

2. Add the onion to the pot and cook over medium heat until it begins to soften, about 5 minutes. Add the broth, parsnips, potatoes, salt, and enough water to just cover the vegetables. Bring to a boil, then reduce the heat to medium-low and cook,

covered, until the parsnips and potatoes are tender, about 15 minutes.

3. If you'd like, use a potato masher to mash about one-quarter of the soup in the pot to thicken the chowder. Add the half-and-half and cook over very low heat for 2 minutes to blend the flavors. Season with pepper and additional salt if needed. Let the chowder sit at cool room temperature for at least an hour or, better yet, refrigerate overnight.

4. Reheat over very low heat so the chowder does not curdle, adding a bit more liquid if it seems too thick. Ladle into bowls and sprinkle with the parsley. Pass the pork bits (reheated in the microwave) for sprinkling on the chowder if desired.

NOTE
If you're using bacon it should produce enough of its own fat, so there's no need to cook it in butter. After removing the cooked bits, you should have about 2 tablespoons of bacon fat; discard any excess and add 2 tablespoons butter to make a total of 4 table-spoons fat.

BROCCOLI and CHEDDAR CHOWDER

This chowder is based on one that I ate when I was researching a story on potatoes in Maine's Aroostook County. The robust primary flavors — bacon, potatoes, broccoli, and cheddar cheese — marry perfectly with one another. It's a nice simple chowder, good for a weeknight meal, and it's great in summer with Shingled Tomato and Nectarine Salad with Olive Vinaigrette (page 103). Oversize Oatmeal-Raisin Cookies (page 123) make an ideal dessert.

4 SERVINGS

4 ounces bacon, cut into ½-inch pieces (about 1 cup)

1 large onion, chopped

2 garlic cloves, finely chopped

1 teaspoon dry mustard

1 (32-ounce) carton shelf-stable chicken broth

1 cup water

1¼ pounds all-purpose potatoes, peeled and diced (about 3¾ cups)

½ teaspoon salt, plus more if needed

1 pound broccoli florets (about 5 cups)

2 cups half-and-half

1½ cups shredded cheddar cheese

¼ teaspoon grated nutmeg

Freshly ground black pepper

1. Cook the bacon in a large heavy soup pot or Dutch oven over medium-low heat until crisp and the fat is rendered, 10 to 15 minutes. Add the onion and cook over medium heat until it begins to soften, about 5 minutes.

2. Add the garlic and mustard and cook, stirring, for 1 minute. Add the broth and water along with the potatoes and salt, and bring to a boil. Reduce the heat to low and cook, covered, until the potatoes are tender, about 15 minutes. Add the broccoli and cook for 4 minutes longer.

3. Stir in the half-and-half and add the cheese by handfuls, stirring over very low heat until it melts. Season with the nutmeg and pepper to taste; it may not need salt because the bacon and cheese are salty. This chowder is best eaten the same day so the broccoli does not discolor, but it can sit at cool room temperature for an hour or two.

4. If reheating, warm over very low heat so the chowder does not curdle. Ladle into bowls and serve.

2 SPLENDID SEAFOOD STEWS
AND A BISQUE

AMERICAN BOUILLABAISSE
with GARLIC TOASTS
and SRIRACHA ROUILLE

5 cups water

1 teaspoon salt, plus more if needed

2 (1½-pound) live lobsters, rinsed (see Note)

5 tablespoons olive oil

1 large onion, chopped

2 leeks, cleaned, cut in half lengthwise, and thinly sliced (white and pale green parts only)

4 garlic cloves, finely chopped

1 tablespoon fennel seeds

¾ teaspoon saffron threads

1 cup dry white wine

1 (14½-ounce) can diced tomatoes with juice

6 sprigs flat-leaf parsley

24 mussels, scrubbed

1½ pounds haddock or other flaky white fish such as cod or sea bass, cut into 4-inch chunks

1 pound shelled and deveined large shrimp

½ cup torn basil leaves

Freshly ground black pepper

The original French bouillabaisse was created in the port city of Marseilles and is concocted of all manner of native fish and shellfish. This is an American version, using lobsters and mussels and our own local fish. Bouillabaisse is traditionally served topped with a garlic *croûte* that is spread with rouille, a spicy red pepper mayonnaise, but I saw no real reason to go to the trouble of making a homemade mayo, especially now that we have ready access to sriracha, a Southeast Asia–style sauce, and smoked paprika.

Complete this special meal with Baby Kale Salad with Pine Nuts (page 108) and Bittersweet Chocolate-Pecan Tart (page 111).

6 SERVINGS

1. Bring the water to a boil in a large soup pot and add the salt. Add the lobsters, cover, and return to a boil. Cook, covered, over medium-low heat until the lobsters are bright red and fully cooked, 14 to 17 minutes. (Hard-shell lobsters will take the longer cooking time.) Use tongs to remove the lobsters to a bowl, leaving the cooking liquid in the pot. ⟳

2. Remove the claws and tails and set aside, rinse off most of the tomalley (green material) from the lobster bodies, and return the bodies to the pot. Return to a boil, reduce the heat to low, and cook, uncovered, for 15 minutes. Strain through a medium-mesh strainer into a bowl. Measure out 4 cups of broth, which will be tinted a pretty pale green from the lobster bodies. Meanwhile, pick out the lobster claw and tail meat and refrigerate. (This can be done up to 24 hours ahead.)

3. Heat the oil in a large heavy soup pot or Dutch oven. Add the onion and leeks and cook over medium heat until they begin to soften, about 5 minutes. Add the garlic, fennel, and saffron, and cook, stirring frequently, for 2 minutes longer.

4. Add the wine, raise the heat to high, and boil briskly until the liquid is reduced by about half, about 4 minutes. Add the reserved lobster broth, tomatoes, and parsley, and cook over medium heat, uncovered, for about 10 minutes to blend the flavors. (This base can be made up to 24 hours ahead. Cover and refrigerate.)

5. Reheat the base if necessary. Add the mussels and cook, covered, over medium heat until they begin to open, 4 to 8 minutes, depending on size. Add the fish and cook until it is cooked through, about 4 minutes. Add the shrimp and remove the pot from the heat to finish cooking. Stir in the basil and season with pepper and additional salt if needed. The stew can sit for up to an hour at cool room temperature. Reheat gently.

6. Meanwhile, split the reserved lobster tails, remove the black intestinal veins, and cut the meat into 1½-inch pieces. Slice the reserved claw meat in half horizontally to make double the number of claw shapes. When ready to serve, gently reheat the lobster meat in a saucepan with a bit of the broth from the stew.

7. Ladle the stew into shallow bowls and distribute the lobster more or less evenly over the top. Top each portion with a garlic toast and pass the sriracha rouille (recipes follow) at the table to spread on the toasts and/or stir into the soup.

"Of soup and love, the first is best."
— Spanish proverb

You can also use ½ pound of chopped, picked-out lobster meat and 4 cups seafood broth, clam juice, or a combination of clam juice and water. Canned seafood broth can usually be found with the canned chicken and beef broth in the supermarket; bottled clam juice is usually shelved with the canned fish.

SRIRACHA ROUILLE

1 large garlic clove
½ teaspoon kosher salt
¾ cup prepared mayonnaise
1 tablespoon sriracha, plus more if needed
1 teaspoon smoked paprika

Coarsely chop the garlic with the salt, then use the flat side of the knife blade to mash the mixture into a paste. Combine the garlic and salt paste, mayonnaise, sriracha, and paprika in a small bowl and whisk to blend. Taste and add more sriracha if you want a seriously spicy sauce. Cover and refrigerate for at least 2 hours to blend the flavors. (The sauce will keep for up to about a week in the refrigerator.)

GARLIC TOASTS

4 tablespoons extra-virgin olive oil
1 large garlic clove, finely chopped
12–18 (depending on diameter) thick slices crusty French bread

1. Preheat the oven to 375°F/190°C.

2. Combine the oil and garlic in a small bowl and let stand for at least 15 minutes.

3. Arrange the bread in a single layer on one or two baking sheets, brush with the garlic oil, and bake in the preheated oven for 7 to 10 minutes, or until golden brown.

CREOLE SEAFOOD GUMBO

⅓ cup vegetable oil

½ cup all-purpose flour

1 large onion, chopped

1 green bell pepper, seeded and chopped

2 celery stalks, chopped

1 (10-ounce) package frozen okra, trimmed and thinly sliced

4 garlic cloves, finely chopped

2 teaspoons dried thyme

2 bay leaves

4 cups seafood broth (see Note)

2–3 cups water

½ teaspoon cayenne pepper

12 ounces andouille or other smoked sausage such as kielbasa, cut into ¼-inch-thick slices

1 pound shelled and deveined medium or large shrimp (see Note)

8 ounces crabmeat, picked over to remove cartilage

1 pint shucked oysters with their liquor

1 tablespoon filé powder

Salt and freshly ground black pepper

½ cup thinly sliced scallions

½ cup chopped flat-leaf parsley

4 cups hot cooked white rice

Oh, how I love gumbo! I make it every year for a Mardi Gras party, using a version of the recipe developed for my cookbook *The Best of New Orleans* (Collins, 1994). Some Creole gumbos are thickened with okra, and some with filé powder (ground sassafras leaves), but this uses both, for flavor as well as texture. Add a basket of Crusty Skillet Cornbread (page 89); Orange, Radish, and Basil Salad (page 101); and Sour Lemon Tart in a Graham Cracker Crust (page 121) to complete a grand and glorious meal.

8 SERVINGS

1. Heat the oil in a large heavy soup pot. Add the flour and cook over medium heat, stirring with a wooden spoon almost constantly until the roux is a deep reddish brown and has a toasty aroma, about 15 minutes. (Be very careful of spattering; hot roux can cause severe burns.) Add the onion, bell pepper, celery, okra, garlic, thyme, and bay leaves, and cook over medium heat until the vegetables are soft and lightly browned, about 10 minutes.

2. Add the seafood broth, 2 cups of the water, cayenne, and sausage, and bring to a boil. Reduce the heat to medium-low and cook, uncovered, for 20 minutes.

3. Add the shrimp, crabmeat, and oysters, and cook over medium heat until the oysters begin to shrink and the edges curl, about 5 minutes. Remove from the heat, stir in the filé powder, and season with salt and pepper to taste. Set the gumbo aside at cool room temperature for at least an hour or, better yet, refrigerate for up to 2 days.

4. Reheat gently when ready to serve, adding more water if it seems too thick. Stir in the scallions and parsley. Ladle into bowls, top with a scoop of rice, and serve.

NOTE

If you have shrimp shells, make a quick broth: Combine them in a pot with ½ teaspoon salt and 4 cups water. Bring to a boil, then reduce the heat to low and cook, covered, for 20 minutes. Strain. Or use seafood broth, which can usually be found — in cans or shelf-stable cartons, or in jars as a concentrate — with the canned chicken and beef broth in the supermarket.

OYSTERS ROCKEFELLER STEW

4 ounces bacon, cut into
½-inch pieces (about 1 cup)

2 tablespoons butter, plus
more if needed

1 large leek, cleaned, cut in
half lengthwise, and thinly
sliced (white and pale green
parts only)

1 large celery stalk, finely
chopped

⅛ teaspoon cayenne pepper

2 cups bottled clam juice or
seafood broth (see Note)

1 cup water, plus more if
needed

2 pints shucked oysters with
their liquor, cut in half if
very large

2 teaspoons Worcestershire
sauce

2 cups heavy cream

Salt and freshly ground
black pepper

4 ounces baby spinach, thinly
sliced (about 3 cups)

2 tablespoons medium-dry
sherry

Oysters Rockefeller — oysters with a rich-as-Rockefeller topping made with butter and bacon and brightened with chopped spinach — is a New Orleans classic. When Melanie Barnard and I did a book called *Let's Eat In*, we added these elements to a classic oyster stew and decided it could be a meal unto itself. Add Brussels Sprout Slaw (page 100), oyster crackers or toasted common crackers, and a plate of Black Pepper Brownies (page 119) for a lovely supper.

4 SERVINGS

1. Cook the bacon in a large heavy soup pot or Dutch oven over medium-low heat until crisp and the fat is rendered, 10 to 15 minutes. Remove the cooked bits with a slotted spoon, drain on paper towels, and reserve. You should have 2 tablespoons of fat in the pot; if there is too much, pour some off, or if there is too little, make up the difference with additional butter.

2. Add the butter to the pot and cook the leek and celery over medium heat until softened but not browned, about 8 minutes. Stir in the cayenne. Add the clam juice and water and bring just to a simmer.

3. Add the oysters and the Worcestershire and cook over low heat until the edges of the oysters begin to shrink and curl at the edges, about 2 minutes. Stir in the cream and season with salt and black pepper to taste. If there is not enough liquid,

add a bit more water. Let sit at cool room temperature for at least an hour, or refrigerate overnight.

4. Reheat over very low heat so the stew does not curdle, stir in the spinach, and cook for 2 minutes, or until the spinach wilts. Stir in the sherry, ladle into soup bowls, sprinkle with the reserved bacon, and serve.

NOTE

Bottled clam juice is usually shelved with the canned fish in the supermarket. Seafood broth — in cans or shelf-stable cartons, or in jars as a concentrate — can usually be found with the canned chicken and beef broth.

CHOWDER CRACKERS

Early New Englanders thickened their chowders with ship's biscuit, also known as hardtack, and even though chowders are now thickened with potatoes, crisp crackers are still an ideal accompaniment to a creamy chowder. Round, puffy, hollow common crackers, which have been made in Vermont for almost 200 years, are a wonderful complement to chowder, especially when split and toasted. They can be ordered from vermontcommonfoods.com. Nabisco's Crown Pilot crackers, another crisp, hard cracker, were discontinued in 2008, much to the disappointment — nay, utter dismay — of chowder lovers everywhere. Small oyster crackers — the kind that are served in little bags with a cup of chowder in restaurants — are also a classic garnish.

PORTUGUESE SEAFOOD STEW with CHOURIÇO

STEW

- 6 tablespoons olive oil
- 12 ounces *chouriço,* cut into ½-inch slices
- 2 green bell peppers, seeded and chopped
- 2 onions, chopped
- 4 garlic cloves, finely chopped
- 2 bay leaves, broken in half
- 1 cup dry white wine
- 3 cups bottled clam juice or seafood broth (see Note)
- 1 (14½-ounce) can tomato sauce or purée
- 1 cup water, plus more if needed
- 2 teaspoons smoked paprika
- 30 mussels, scrubbed (about 1¼ pounds)
- 12–18 littleneck clams, scrubbed (see Note)
- 2 pounds firm boneless fish such as haddock or cod, cut into 3-inch chunks
  Freshly ground black pepper
  Salt, if needed
  MORE ⊖

Called *caldeirada* in Portuguese after the large earthenware vessel it's cooked in, this magnificent fishermen's stew is one of Portugal's supreme contributions to world cuisine. *Chouriço,* the peppery smoked Portuguese sausage, lends its distinctive flavor, but if you can't find it you can use any garlicky cooked sausage, such as kielbasa. The stew is finished with a shower of Portuguese gremolata — roasted diced potatoes tossed with cilantro (an often-used herb in Portuguese cooking), parsley, and lemon. Add Baby Kale Salad with Pine Nuts (page 108), some crusty Portuguese bread to mop up the sauce, and Lemon Sponge Pudding Cake (page 113) for dessert.

5–6 SERVINGS

1. For the stew, heat the oil in a very large, heavy soup pot or Dutch oven. Add the *chouriço* and green bell peppers and cook over medium heat until the mixture browns lightly, about 5 minutes. Remove with a slotted spoon, leaving the drippings in the pot. Add the onions, garlic, and bay leaves, and cook over medium heat until the onion begins to soften, about 5 minutes. ⊖

1¾ pounds all-purpose potatoes, unpeeled, cut in ½-
inch dice (about 5½ cups)

3 tablespoons olive oil

1 teaspoon salt

2 teaspoons grated lemon
zest

6 tablespoons fresh lemon
juice

½ cup chopped flat-leaf
parsley

½ cup chopped cilantro

Freshly ground black pepper

LINGUICA AND CHOURIÇO

These two glorious staples of Portuguese-American cookery are smoked pork sausages redolent of garlic and paprika. *Chouriço,* which is spicier, is usually about 1½ inches in diameter and hence is juicier; linguica is drier and skinnier, but the two can be used more or less interchangeably. There is also a Spanish sausage called chorizo, which can be somewhat similar and can often be substituted for the Portuguese varieties.

---

2. Add the wine, raise the heat to high, and cook until reduced by about half, about 4 minutes. Add the clam juice, tomato sauce, water, and paprika, and bring to a boil. Reduce the heat to medium and cook, covered, for 15 minutes to blend the flavors. Return the sausage and bell peppers to the sauce and heat through. (This base can be made a day ahead; cover and refrigerate.)

3. Reheat the base if necessary. Add the mussels and clams to the pot and cook, covered, over medium heat until they begin to open, about 5 minutes. Add the fish and continue cooking, covered, until all the bivalves are open and the fish is opaque, about 5 minutes. Season with pepper and, if needed, salt (it will probably not be needed; the sausage and clam juice are salty). Add a bit more water if the stew is not liquid enough. The stew can sit at cool room temperature for up to an hour.

4. Meanwhile, for the gremolata, preheat the oven to 375°F/190°C. On one or two rimmed baking sheets, toss the potatoes with the oil and salt and spread into a more or less even layer. Roast in the preheated oven for 25 to 30 minutes, or until the potatoes are lightly browned and tender when pierced with a knife. Transfer to a bowl. (Can be made up to 4 hours ahead and held at room temperature. Reheat for a minute or two in the microwave.) Toss the potatoes with the lemon zest, lemon juice, parsley, and cilantro, and season with pepper to taste.

5. Reheat the stew gently and ladle into shallow bowls, making sure each serving gets an equal number of mussels/clams. Pass the gremolata separately so that guests can sprinkle it on their stew.

NOTE

Bottled clam juice is usually shelved with the canned fish in the supermarket; seafood broth — in cans or shelf-stable cartons, or in jars as a concentrate — can usually be found with the canned chicken and beef broth. If you can't get clams, use all mussels.

PENOBSCOT BAY SCALLOP STEW

A very traditional scallop stew is white on white and completely unadorned, tasting of nothing more than its essential ingredients — fresh sweet scallops, pure creamery milk or cream, and butter. Here's a slight variation, treated to a contemporary "face-lift" but with its beautiful (and delicious) soul intact. Serve the stew with Winter Greens with Apple, Walnuts, and Blue Cheese (page 107); Red Pepper–Scallion Pita Toasts (page 91); and Dark and Sticky Candied Gingerbread (page 129).

4 SERVINGS

2 cups heavy cream

2 cups bottled clam juice or seafood broth (see Note)

1 small onion, quartered

1 leafy celery top

4 sprigs flat-leaf parsley, including stems

1 teaspoon salt, plus more if needed

1 large bay leaf, broken in half

¼ cup finely chopped celery

1¾ pounds sea scallops

2 tablespoons snipped chives or green parts of scallions

1 tablespoon chopped fresh tarragon or 1 teaspoon dried

1 tablespoon chopped fresh marjoram or 1 teaspoon dried

¼ teaspoon cayenne pepper

5 tablespoons butter

Freshly ground black pepper

1. Combine the cream, clam juice, onion, celery top, parsley, salt, and bay leaf in a large saucepan and heat over medium-low heat just until bubbles form around the edges. Remove from the heat, cover, and let stand for 15 minutes to infuse the cream with the seasoning vegetables. Strain out the vegetables and discard, returning the flavored cream to the saucepan.

2. Add the chopped celery to the flavored cream and cook, covered, over low heat until it softens slightly, about 5 minutes.

3. Remove the side hinges from the scallops and, if large, cut them into halves or quarters. Add the scallops, chives, tarragon, marjoram, and cayenne to the cream mixture. Cook gently over low heat, uncovered, until the scallops are just cooked through, about 3 minutes. Add the butter, stirring until it melts. Season with black pepper and additional salt if needed. Let sit at cool room temperature for at least an hour, or refrigerate overnight.

4. Reheat the stew very gently, ladle into shallow soup bowls, and serve.

NOTE
Bottled clam juice is usually shelved with the canned fish in the supermarket; seafood broth — in cans or shelf-stable cartons, or in jars as a concentrate — can usually be found with the canned chicken and beef broth.

The REAL DEAL LOBSTER BISQUE

LOBSTER BROTH

- 7 cups water
- 1 teaspoon salt
- 2 (1½-pound) live lobsters, rinsed
- 3 tablespoons butter

BISQUE

- 5 tablespoons butter
- 1 medium onion, chopped
- 1 carrot, finely chopped
- 1 large garlic clove, finely chopped
- ¼ cup all-purpose flour
- 1 cup dry white wine
- 2 tablespoons tomato paste
- 1 tablespoon chopped fresh thyme
- 1 bay leaf, broken in half
- 1 cup heavy cream
- 2 tablespoons cream sherry
- Salt and freshly ground black pepper

If you're craving lobster bisque — and are looking for a challenging weekend cooking project — this is the recipe for you. It's based on one I developed in collaboration with *Fine Cooking* magazine, and all the labor involved (primarily crushing and sautéing the shells) illustrates the lengths to which serious chefs will go in order to create a dish with this much depth of flavor. There really are no shortcuts.

Because it's not ultra-rich, the bisque is really not filling enough to stand as a main course, but . . . as a first course for an ultra-special dinner, it's a wow.

5–6 FIRST-COURSE SERVINGS

1. For the broth, bring the water to a boil in a large soup pot and add the salt. Add the lobsters, cover, and return to a boil. Cook, covered, over medium-low heat until the lobsters are bright red and fully cooked, 14 to 17 minutes. (Hard-shell lobsters will take the longer cooking time.) Use tongs to remove the lobsters to a bowl, leaving the cooking liquid in the pot. Measure out 6 cups of the cooking liquid and reserve. Remove the lobster tails and claws and pick out the meat. Slice the tails lengthwise and remove the black intestinal vein. Dice *half* the meat and set aside for garnish; coarsely chop the remaining meat. Reserve the empty shells. ➔

2. Rinse most of the tomalley out of the upper bodies, split them lengthwise, use your fingers to remove the innards, and reserve the bodies. Using kitchen shears or a large chef's knife, break the empty tail and claw shells into 1- to 2-inch pieces. Put the pieces in a heavy ziplock bag and use a large mallet or the bottom of a small heavy pot to flatten the shells.

3. Melt the butter in a large heavy pot. Add the crushed shells and reserved lobster bodies and cook over medium heat, stirring occasionally, until they begin to blister, about 5 minutes. Add the 6 cups reserved cooking liquid and bring to a boil. Reduce the heat to medium-low and cook, uncovered, for 30 minutes, skimming off any foam that rises to the surface. Strain through a medium-mesh sieve. You should have 4 cups of broth; if there is too much, continue cooking to reduce, or, if there is too little, add water to make up the difference. (The broth can be made a day ahead and refrigerated or frozen.)

4. For the bisque, melt the butter in a large heavy soup pot. Add the onion, carrot, and garlic, and cook over medium heat until softened, about 10 minutes. Sprinkle on the flour and cook, whisking, until pale golden and bubbly, about 2 minutes.

5. Whisk in the lobster broth, wine, tomato paste, thyme, and bay leaf, and bring to a boil. Cook, uncovered, over medium heat until the liquid is slightly reduced, about 4 minutes. Add the reserved chopped lobster meat and cook for 2 minutes. Remove the bay leaf. Cool the mixture slightly.

6. Purée the mixture with an immersion blender or in a standing blender in batches (a food processor does not do a good job with this large a proportion of liquid) until smooth. Strain through a medium-mesh sieve back into the pot, pushing hard on the solids. Stir in the cream and sherry, season with salt and pepper to taste, and cook the bisque over medium-low heat until lightly thickened, about 10 minutes. (The bisque can be made up to a day ahead. Refrigerate the soup and garnish separately.)

7. If reheating, warm gently. Ladle into bowls, garnish with the reserved diced lobster meat, and serve.

CHOWDER AGEISM

"Aging brings out flavor no spices or sudden terrific heat can reach. A lobster stew, made and set aside for two days tastes like something the mermaids might think up after they have sat out in the white Maine surf for three hours of a sun-drenched day and sung all their shrillest and most silvery songs."

— Robert P. Tristram Coffin, *Maine Cooking*

TRADITIONAL LOBSTER STEW

Classically nothing more than lobster, butter, milk and/or cream, and a dash of paprika, lobster stew harkens back to early days when stewing referred simply to the process of simmering in a liquid, and a stew did not necessarily contain various other ingredients. Returning the lobster bodies to the stew enriches its flavor, and the aging process, which is essential here, develops a brew that is fully infused with lobster. It can be the featured centerpiece of a summer supper, accompanied, perhaps, by Grilled Summer Vegetable Salad with Balsamic Drizzle (page 104), Kale Toasts (page 96), and Lattice-Top Blueberry Pie (page 114).

4 SERVINGS

2 teaspoons salt, plus more if needed

3 live lobsters (1¼–1½ pounds each), rinsed

6 tablespoons butter

¾ cup dry white wine

2 teaspoons paprika

2 cups heavy cream

3 cups whole milk

Sprinkling of snipped fresh chives (heretical, but nice)

1. Fill a large pot with about 2 inches of water, add the salt, and bring to a boil. Add the lobsters, reduce the heat to medium, and cook, covered, until the lobsters are bright red and fully cooked, 14 to 17 minutes. (Hard-shell lobsters will take the longer cooking time.)

2. Drain the lobsters, and when cool enough to handle, crack the tails and claws over a bowl, catching and saving as much juice as you can. Pull out the meat, discard the intestinal veins, and chop the meat into 1-inch chunks. Add to the bowl with the reserved juices. Scoop the green tomalley out of the bodies and reserve a tablespoon or two, discarding the rest. (Although the tomalley looks unappetizing at this point, the color will not affect the finished stew. See the box on page 84.) Reserve two of the lobster bodies. →

3. Melt the butter in a large heavy soup pot or Dutch oven. Add the reserved tomalley and cook over medium heat, stirring frequently, for 5 minutes. Add the wine, raise the heat to high, and boil briskly until the liquid is reduced by about half, about 4 minutes. Add the reserved lobster meat and juices and sprinkle on the paprika.

4. Reduce the heat to low and slowly add the cream and milk, stirring constantly. Place the reserved lobster bodies in the stew and cook over very low heat for 2 minutes. Cool to room temperature and refrigerate for at least 6 hours or overnight.

5. Remove and discard the lobster bodies. Reheat the stew over very low heat, stirring often so it does not curdle. Taste for seasoning, adding salt if needed. Ladle into bowls, sprinkle with the chives if desired, and serve.

TOMALLEY

"It is the green stuff in the central core of the lobster which is the quintessence of the creature and the nearest we mortals can come to the ambrosia of the Greek gods. It is the tomalley. People have been known to shy away from this substance and put it gingerly to one side. . . Multiply all the taste in the lobster by ten, by twenty, and you have this emerald delicacy which tops all flavors of the world."
— Robert P. Tristram Coffin, *Maine Cooking*

3 ACCOMPANYING BREADS

NARRAGANSETT CLAM FRITTERS

Clam fritters (also known as clam cakes) are traditionally served in Rhode Island and South Coast Massachusetts as an accompaniment to that region's famous Classic Rhode Island Clear Clam Chowder (page 21). My friend Susan Maloney, who grew up in Fall River, Massachusetts, near Narragansett Bay, always extolled her Aunt Phyllis Corcoran's fritters. When I finally got around to making her recipe, I had to agree that these are the very best clam cakes I've ever eaten. The mixture is proportioned exactly right — a high concentration of chopped clams suspended in a batter that fries up light and crispy every time.

MAKES ABOUT 3 DOZEN FRITTERS (6–8 SERVINGS)

1 egg

3 tablespoons vegetable oil, plus more for frying

¾ cup bottled clam juice or clam liquor drained from clams

¼ cup milk

1½ cups all-purpose flour

2 teaspoons baking powder

½ teaspoon salt, plus more if needed

¼ teaspoon black pepper

1 cup finely chopped drained hard-shell clams

Cider vinegar or lemon wedges

Liquid hot pepper sauce

1. Whisk the egg and oil in a small bowl until blended. Whisk in the clam juice and milk.

2. Combine the flour, baking powder, salt, and pepper in a large bowl and whisk to blend. Whisk in the egg mixture just until blended and stir in the clams. The batter should be the consistency of thick cake batter. Adjust by adding a little more flour or liquid as needed.

3. Heat 2 inches of oil in a large deep skillet to 370°F/190°C, or until a drop of batter sizzles when dropped on the surface. Dip a teaspoon into the oil (see Note), then use it to spoon out one rounded spoonful of batter and drop into the hot fat. Cook for 2 to 3 minutes, turning once with tongs, until puffed and golden. Taste this first fritter for seasoning, adding more salt and pepper to the batter if needed. If the fritter seems dense, add a bit more liquid. Continue frying the fritters, a few at a time, until all the batter is used. Drain on paper towels. $\rightarrow$

4. Pass vinegar or lemon wedges and the hot sauce for seasoning the clam cakes.

NOTE

I like to use a long-handled iced-tea spoon to portion out the batter. It keeps your hands from getting too close to the hot oil, and it also creates a nicely shaped and sized fritter.

CLAM CAKES GALORE

The annual Newport Chowder Festival features a Clam Cake Chow-Down, an eating contest to test the mettle of participants willing to down clam fritter after clam fritter. The winner (usually a large male) is crowned King of Clam Cakes.

CRUSTY SKILLET CORNBREAD

Cornbread accompanies almost any chowder beautifully, and heating a cast-iron skillet or metal baking pan before the batter goes in results in cornbread with a nice crisp bottom crust. Serve the cornbread with more butter, and honey, if you like.

6 SERVINGS

4 tablespoons unsalted butter
1 tablespoon vegetable oil
1¼ cups all-purpose flour
¾ cup yellow cornmeal
2 tablespoons sugar
1 tablespoon baking powder
1 teaspoon salt
1 egg
1 cup whole or low-fat milk

> "Without bread all is misery."
> — William Cobbett

1. Preheat the oven to 425°F/220°C.

2. Melt the butter in a 9-inch cast-iron skillet (see Note) over medium heat, and pour most of the melted butter into a small bowl. Add the vegetable oil to the pan and heat until hot but not scorching. The batter should sizzle when it goes into the pan.

3. Meanwhile, whisk the flour with the cornmeal, sugar, baking powder, and salt in a medium bowl.

4. Add the egg and milk to the butter in the small bowl and whisk to blend. Pour the milk mixture into the flour mixture and stir gently but thoroughly to combine. Scrape the batter into the hot pan and smooth the top. Wear an oven mitt to transfer the pan to the oven.

5. Bake in the preheated oven until the bread is pale golden brown and a tester inserted in the center comes out clean, 15 to 18 minutes. Cut into wedges and serve hot.

NOTE

Measure the bottom of the skillet, which can be between about 8¾ and 9½ inches in diameter. If using the larger pan, test the bread after the minimum baking time. You can also bake this in a 9-inch square metal baking pan, following the same directions.

RED PEPPER-SCALLION PITA TOASTS

These simple-to-make toasts look like a Paul Klee painting, adding a shot of delicious color that makes them the ideal accompaniment to any creamy chowder or seafood stew.

4–6 SERVINGS

8 (4½-inch) pita breads

½ red bell pepper, very thinly sliced lengthwise and then halved crosswise to make 1½-inch strips (about 1 cup)

½ cup thinly sliced scallions

6 tablespoons extra-virgin olive oil

Freshly ground black pepper

Flaky sea salt, such as Maldon salt (see Note)

> "Bread is like dresses, hats, and shoes — in other words, essential!"
> — Emily Post

1. Split the pita breads around their circumference using kitchen scissors or a serrated knife and arrange cut side up on two baking sheets. Arrange 3 or 4 strips of bell pepper on each round and scatter with scallions. (Can be made several hours ahead. Cover and hold at room temperature.)

2. Preheat the oven to 400°F/200°C.

3. Drizzle the breads with the oil. (The easiest way to do this is to dip a brush in oil and shake gently over the breads.) Grind black pepper over the top.

4. Bake in the preheated oven until the bread is tinged with brown on the edges and golden in the center, 6 to 7 minutes. Remove from the oven and sprinkle lightly with the salt (if the flakes are large, grind a bit with your fingertips). Cut the breads in half and serve immediately in a napkin-lined basket.

NOTE

There are several types of flaky sea salt, including Maldon salt. Produced in England, Maldon salt has soft flakes and is beloved by chefs for its pure flavor, absence of bitterness, and extreme saltiness.

ROSEMARY-ONION FOCACCIA

Baking these focaccia in cake pans makes for an evenly shaped loaf, and the heat of the pan turns the sides of the bread crusty and golden. As a shortcut, you can buy pizza dough and add the onion and rosemary topping. Serve the flatbread in wedges with any chowder.

MAKES 2 LOAVES

DOUGH

- 1 cup warm water (105–115°F/40–45°C)
- 1 package active dry yeast (2¼ teaspoons)
- 1 teaspoon sugar
- ¼ cup extra-virgin olive oil
- 2 teaspoons kosher salt, plus about 1 teaspoon additional salt for sprinkling
- 2¾ cups all-purpose flour, plus additional tablespoons as needed

FINISHING AND TOPPING

- 2 tablespoons extra-virgin olive oil
- ½ medium yellow onion, very thinly sliced (about ¾ cup)
- 2 tablespoons coarsely chopped fresh rosemary
- ¼ teaspoon red pepper flakes
- ¾ teaspoon kosher salt

1. For the dough, pour the warm water into a large mixing bowl or the bowl of a standing mixer. Sprinkle the yeast over the water, add the sugar, and let stand until foamy, about 5 minutes.

2. Stir the oil and salt into the yeast mixture. Stir in the flour until a soft dough forms. Turn out onto a floured board and knead until the dough is smooth and elastic, about 10 minutes, or knead in a stand mixer with a dough hook, about 5 minutes. Add 1 or 2 more tablespoons of flour if the dough is too sticky. You want a soft but workable dough. Place in a large oiled bowl, cover with plastic wrap, and let rise in a warm place until doubled in bulk, 1 to 1½ hours.

3. Use about 1 tablespoon of the Finishing and Topping oil to grease two 9-inch round cake pans. Punch down the dough, divide into two balls, and transfer to the prepared pans. Cover loosely with plastic wrap and let rest for 30 minutes. Pat the dough evenly into the pans and let rest, loosely covered, until slightly puffy, at least 30 minutes.

4. Preheat the oven to 450°F/230°C.

5. Make dimples in the surface of the dough with your fingertips and drizzle with the remaining 1 tablespoon oil. ⊙

Arrange the onion slivers atop the breads, scatter with the rosemary, and sprinkle with the pepper flakes and salt.

6. Bake in the preheated oven for 10 minutes. Reduce the heat to 400°F/200°C and continue baking until the focaccia are golden brown and the onion is tinged with char, 20 to 25 minutes longer. Turn out on a rack to cool. The loaves can be baked several hours ahead of serving and also freeze well. To reheat, wrap in foil and place in a preheated 375°F/190°C oven for 10 to 15 minutes before serving.

SALT and PEPPER BISCUITS

These are not your fluffy mile-high biscuits but are designed to rise to about an inch and have an almost crisp bite — something akin to a cracker. They're an ideal accompaniment to chowders of any stripe. Black pepper adds a subtle bite to the dough, and a generous sprinkling of flaky sea salt is a lovely final fillip.

MAKES ABOUT 16 BISCUITS

2 cups all-purpose flour

1 teaspoon table salt

½ teaspoon black pepper

2 teaspoons baking powder

1 teaspoon sugar

3 tablespoons cold unsalted butter, cut into chunks

3 tablespoons cold vegetable shortening, cut into chunks

¾ cup cold whole milk, plus about 1 tablespoon for brushing the biscuit tops

1 teaspoon flaky sea salt, such as Maldon salt (see Note), for sprinkling

1. Preheat the oven to 400°F/200°C.

2. In a food processor, combine the flour, table salt, pepper, baking powder, and sugar, and pulse to blend. Distribute the chunks of butter and shortening over the flour and pulse 8 to 10 times, until most of the shortening is about the size of peas. Slowly pour the ¾ cup milk through the feed tube, pulsing until the dough begins to clump together. (To make by hand, whisk together the dry ingredients in a large bowl. Work the butter and shortening in with your fingertips until most of the shortening is about the size of peas. Add the milk all at once and stir with a fork to make a soft dough.)

3. Turn the dough out onto a lightly floured board, gather into a ball, and knead 5 to 10 times until smooth. Roll to a scant ½-inch thickness. Using a 2-inch cutter or a floured glass, cut the biscuits and place on an ungreased baking sheet. Reroll the scraps and cut once. (The biscuits can be shaped up to 3 hours ahead. Refrigerate, loosely covered.)

4. Using about 1 tablespoon of milk, brush the biscuit tops and sprinkle with the sea salt. Bake in the preheated oven until the biscuits are pale golden and have risen, 12 to 15 minutes. Serve hot or warm. (Can be made a few hours ahead. If making ahead, underbake slightly and reheat in the oven at 400°F/200°C for 5 minutes.)

NOTE

There are several types of flaky sea salt, including Maldon salt. Produced in England, Maldon salt has soft flakes and is beloved by chefs for its pure flavor, absence of bitterness, and extreme saltiness.

KALE TOASTS

Earthy, slightly bitter kale, enlivened with garlic and mellowed with good olive oil, is puréed and spread on toasted country bread. These toasts make an ideal accompaniment to many seafood chowders, including, especially, Lobster and Sweet Corn Chowder (page 37).

4–6 SERVINGS

6 tablespoons fruity olive oil

1 large or 2 small garlic cloves, minced

1 large bunch kale (about 12 ounces), tough bottom stems removed, leaves coarsely chopped (about 12 cups)

1 cup water, plus more if needed

¾ teaspoon salt, plus more if needed

¼ teaspoon red pepper flakes

2 tablespoons grated Parmesan cheese

1 tablespoon red wine vinegar

1 (8-ounce) loaf crusty country bread, sliced ½ inch thick

1. Heat 3 tablespoons of the oil in a large deep skillet over medium-high heat. Add the garlic and then add the kale in two or three batches, allowing the leaves to wilt between additions. Toss with tongs. Add the water, salt, and pepper flakes, and bring to a simmer. Cook over medium heat, tossing frequently with the tongs, until very wilted and tender, about 15 minutes. There should be little remaining liquid, but if the kale should begin to scorch, add a bit more water. Cool the kale for 5 minutes.

2. Transfer to a food processor and pulse to make a coarse but spreadable paste, adding a bit more warm water if the mixture seems dry. Add the Parmesan and vinegar and pulse to blend. Season with additional salt if needed. You should have about 1 cup spread. (Can be made up to a day ahead. Reheat slightly in the microwave before using.)

3. Preheat the oven to 375°F/190°C.

4. Arrange the bread in a single layer on a rimmed baking sheet and drizzle or brush lightly with the remaining 3 tablespoons oil. (The easiest way to do this is to dip a brush in oil and shake gently over the slices.) Bake in the preheated oven for 7 to 9 minutes, or until very lightly toasted.

5. Spread the toasted bread with the kale mixture and cut the toasts in half if the slices are large. Arrange on a platter and serve warm or at room temperature.

4 SALADS
ESPECIALLY FOR
CHOWDERS

BEET SALAD on ARUGULA with RICOTTA SALATA

I know, fresh beets are a bit of work to cook and peel, but they are so worth it, especially, in my opinion, when used in a salad. Ricotta salata, which is fresh ricotta that has been pressed, salted, and aged, is somewhat similar to salty, nutty feta cheese and, in fact, the two can be used pretty much interchangeably.

4 SERVINGS

1 pound trimmed beets (about 8 medium beets)

1 small garlic clove

½ teaspoon kosher salt

1½ tablespoons fresh lemon juice

3 tablespoons extra-virgin olive oil

⅛ teaspoon black pepper

3 ounces (3 handfuls) arugula or mesclun mix

4 ounces shaved or crumbled ricotta salata

½ cup imported green olives, pitted or not (your choice)

1. Cook the beets in boiling salted water to cover until tender, 25 to 35 minutes, depending on size, or wrap in foil and roast in the oven at 350°F/180°C for 45 to 60 minutes. When cool, peel and cut into ½-inch dice.

2. Coarsely chop the garlic with the salt, then use the flat side of the knife blade to mash the mixture into a paste. Combine the garlic paste, lemon juice, oil, and pepper in a small bowl and whisk until smooth. Toss the beets with about 2 tablespoons of the dressing and refrigerate until you're ready to assemble the salad.

3. Spread the arugula out on a shallow rimmed platter and drizzle with the remaining dressing. Spread the dressed beets in the center and sprinkle with the cheese. Arrange the olives over the top and serve.

BRUSSELS SPROUT SLAW

Brussels sprouts are tiny cabbages, after all, and when thinly sliced, the green outer leaves and yellow hearts make a lovely, delicate slaw that is wonderful with almost any chowder. This one is enlivened with the rich, salty tang of grated Pecorino Romano cheese.

4 SERVINGS

¼ small red onion, thinly sliced

3 tablespoons fresh lemon juice

1 teaspoon sugar

1 teaspoon whole-grain mustard

2 tablespoons olive oil

½ teaspoon salt

⅛ teaspoon black pepper

8 ounces Brussels sprouts, as large as possible

½ cup grated Pecorino Romano cheese

1. Soak the onion in a bowl of cold water for 15 minutes to rid it of some of its bite. Drain on paper towels.

2. Whisk together the lemon juice, sugar, and mustard in a small bowl. Whisk in the oil, salt, and pepper.

3. Remove any bruised outside leaves from the Brussels sprouts. Holding each sprout by the root end, thinly slice with a sharp knife or slice on a mandoline. Discard the root ends. (You should have about 3½ cups.) Toss with the onion in a medium bowl, gently separating the sprout leaves from one another if necessary. (Can be done up to 4 hours ahead.)

4. When ready to serve, toss the sprouts mixture with the dressing, sprinkle with the cheese, and toss again.

ORANGE, RADISH, and BASIL SALAD

Inspired by a traditional Sicilian antipasto salad, this colorful sweet-salty-bitter composition tastes just as good as it looks. It's lovely with any creamy chowder, especially in winter when one is craving vibrant flavors.

4 SERVINGS

- 5 navel oranges, peeled and sliced crosswise
- 1 large bunch radishes, thinly sliced
- ½ medium red onion, thinly sliced
- 1 cup torn basil leaves, plus sprigs for garnish (optional)
- 3 tablespoons extra-virgin olive oil
- 3 tablespoons sherry or red wine vinegar
- Salt and freshly ground black pepper
- ⅔ cup pitted or unpitted imported black olives, such as Kalamata

1. Spread the oranges, radishes, onion, and basil out on a large platter. Refrigerate until ready to serve.

2. Drizzle with the oil and vinegar, season with salt and pepper to taste, and scatter the olives over the top. Garnish with basil sprigs if desired.

SHINGLED TOMATO and NECTARINE SALAD with OLIVE VINAIGRETTE

Make this beautiful salad during the height of summer, when tomatoes and stone fruits are at their peak of ripeness. It goes perfectly with just about any creamy chowder.

4–6 SERVINGS

1 pound (4 medium) ripe tomatoes, cored and sliced

2 medium nectarines or peaches, pitted and sliced

¼ sweet white onion such as Vidalia, thinly sliced

16 basil leaves

3 tablespoons balsamic vinegar

2 teaspoons Dijon mustard

½ teaspoon salt

¼ teaspoon black pepper

4 tablespoons extra-virgin olive oil

½ cup chopped imported black olives

1. Arrange the tomatoes, nectarines, onion, and basil leaves overlapping on a platter. Refrigerate until ready to serve.

2. Whisk together the vinegar, mustard, salt, and pepper in a small bowl. Whisk in the oil and stir in the olives. (Can be made up to a day ahead. Cover and refrigerate.)

3. Spoon the dressing evenly over the salad and serve.

GRILLED SUMMER VEGETABLE SALAD
with BALSAMIC DRIZZLE

Vegetables are tossed with garlicky olive oil, grilled, interleaved with fresh tomatoes, and drizzled with rich balsamic vinegar. What could be a better accompaniment to a summery seafood chowder?

6 SERVINGS

2 garlic cloves

1 teaspoon salt

6 tablespoons extra-virgin olive oil

2 small or 1 large eggplant (about 1 pound), unpeeled, sliced lengthwise about ½ inch thick

1 large red bell pepper, seeded and cut into 1½-inch-wide pieces

2 medium yellow squash (about 12 ounces), sliced lengthwise about ½ inch thick

2 zucchini (about 12 ounces), sliced lengthwise about ½ inch thick

½ cup coarsely chopped fresh herbs — oregano, parsley, basil, thyme, or a combination, plus sprigs for garnish

1 large or 2 medium ripe tomatoes, cored and sliced

Freshly ground black pepper

3 tablespoons balsamic vinegar

1. Coarsely chop the garlic with the salt, then use the flat side of the knife blade to mash the mixture into a paste. Place in a small bowl and stir in the oil. Set aside for at least 30 minutes to blend the flavors.

2. Build a medium-hot charcoal fire or preheat a gas grill. Combine the eggplant, bell pepper, squash, zucchini, and herbs in a large bowl and toss with the oil to coat well. Grill, turning once or twice, until the eggplant is charred and softened and the other vegetables are nicely charred with grill marks but remain crisp-tender, 10 to 15 minutes.

3. Transfer the vegetables to a platter and cut them into more manageable pieces if desired. Arrange the grilled vegetables with the sliced tomatoes in overlapping layers (shingle-style), grind pepper over, drizzle with the vinegar, and garnish with the herb sprigs. Serve warm, room temperature, or cold.

> **OSCAR WILDE ON SALAD**
>
> "To make a good salad is to be a brilliant diplomatist — the problem is so entirely the same in both cases. To know exactly how much oil one must put with one's vinegar."

VINEGARY CABBAGE SLAW

Sweet-tart vinegary slaw is the perfect foil for many creamy chowders and seafood stews, adding a welcome piquant counterpoint to their creaminess. The carrot, bell pepper, and scallions add beautiful color as well as flavor.

6–8 SERVINGS

½ medium head green cabbage

1 carrot

½ medium red bell pepper, seeded

6 scallions, trimmed

2 tablespoons sugar

¼ cup apple cider vinegar

¼ cup vegetable oil

1 teaspoon salt, plus more if needed

¼ teaspoon celery seeds

Freshly ground black pepper

1. Use the food processor or a large chef's knife to shred the cabbage. (You should have about 7 cups.) Grate the carrot in the food processor or on a box grater (a microplane shreds it too fine). Cut the bell pepper lengthwise into very thin slices and cut the slices in half crosswise to make 1½-inch strips. Cut the scallions into 1-inch lengths, then slice lengthwise into thin strips. Place all the vegetables in a large bowl and toss to mix.

2. Whisk together the sugar and vinegar in a small bowl until most of the sugar is dissolved. Whisk in the oil, salt, and celery seeds. Pour the dressing over the cabbage mixture and toss well. Refrigerate for at least 1 hour or for up to 6 hours.

3. Before serving, drain off any excess liquid, lightly toss the coleslaw, and season with pepper and additional salt if needed.

WINTER GREENS
with APPLE, WALNUTS, and BLUE CHEESE

A classic salad combo — dark greens, crisp apples, nuts, and blue cheese — pairs perfectly with any cold-weather chowder, such as Saint Patrick's Chowder (page 55) or Shrimp, Fennel, and Red Potato Chowder (page 49). Sometimes I present this as a composed salad arranged on individual plates and pass the dressing separately in a small bowl.

6 SERVINGS

VINAIGRETTE

- ¼ cup red wine vinegar
- 1 medium shallot, minced
- ½ teaspoon Worcestershire sauce
- ½ cup olive oil
- ¼ cup crumbled blue cheese
- Salt and freshly ground black pepper

SALAD

- ½ cup coarsely chopped walnuts
- 4 ounces (4 cups) baby spinach
- 1 head frisée or similar greens (6 ounces), torn into bite-size pieces (6 cups)
- 1 Gala or other firm, semi-sweet apple, unpeeled, cored, and cut into match-stick pieces
- ¼ cup crumbled blue cheese

1. For the vinaigrette, whisk together the vinegar, shallot, and Worcestershire in a small bowl or plastic container. Whisk in the oil and blue cheese. Season with salt and pepper to taste. (Can be made up to 2 days ahead. Cover and refrigerate.)

2. Toast the nuts in a small dry skillet over medium heat until fragrant and one shade darker, about 6 minutes. Set aside to cool.

3. Place the spinach and frisée in a salad bowl and toss to combine. Scatter the toasted nuts and apple over the top. Spoon on about ⅓ cup of the dressing and toss gently, adding a bit more dressing if needed. Sprinkle with the blue cheese and put the remaining dressing in a dish for serving.

BABY KALE SALAD
with PINE NUTS

Use the tender baby kale that is now being sold with the other packaged lettuces, or buy a bunch of kale and cut it into fine slivers. The dressing has a secret ingredient that only the cook knows — mashed anchovies — but they give the dressing exactly enough salty intensity to stand up to the assertive greens.

6 SERVINGS

2 ounces (about ⅓ cup) pine nuts

3 anchovy fillets

1 small shallot, finely chopped

4 tablespoons red wine vinegar

4 tablespoons olive oil

2 teaspoons honey

½ teaspoon salt

¼ teaspoon black pepper

6 cups (about 5 ounces) baby kale, torn into bite-size pieces, or thinly sliced kale leaves (see Note)

1 cup halved grape tomatoes

½ cup crumbled feta cheese

1. Toast the pine nuts in a small dry skillet over medium heat, stirring now and then, until one shade darker, about 5 minutes.

2. Chop the anchovies and then mash to a paste with the side of a chef's knife. Combine the anchovy paste, shallot, vinegar, oil, honey, salt, and pepper in a small bowl or covered container and whisk to blend. (The dressing can be made up to 3 days ahead. Cover and refrigerate.)

3. Combine the kale and tomatoes in a salad bowl. Drizzle with the dressing and toss gently. Add the cheese and toss again. Sprinkle with the toasted pine nuts before serving.

NOTE

If you can't get baby kale, the smooth-leaf lacinato (sometimes called Tuscan or dinosaur) kale is usually a bit more tender than the curly variety. Cut it crosswise into fine slivers.

The
5 PERFECT
FINISH

BITTERSWEET CHOCOLATE-PECAN TART

PASTRY

- 1¼ cups all-purpose flour
- 1 teaspoon granulated sugar
- ½ teaspoon salt
- ½ cup (1 stick) cold unsalted butter, cut into small pieces
- 4 tablespoons ice water

FILLING

- 2 eggs
- ½ cup light corn syrup
- ¼ cup granulated sugar
- ¼ teaspoon salt
- 2 tablespoons unsalted butter, melted
- 1 teaspoon vanilla extract
- 1 cup coarsely chopped pecans
- 3 ounces (½ cup) bittersweet chocolate chips

COFFEE CREAM

- ½ cup heavy cream
- 2 tablespoons confectioners' sugar
- 2 teaspoons coffee-flavored liqueur

Oh my, this is such a decadently rich dessert, but there is no more perfect finish to one of the non-cream-based chowders or seafood stews, such as American Bouillabaisse (page 69). The coffee whipped cream provides the final fillip.

6–8 SERVINGS

1. For the pastry, combine the flour, granulated sugar, and salt in a food processor and pulse to blend. Add the butter and pulse until the butter is about the size of peas. Sprinkle with the ice water and pulse, stopping when the dough begins to clump together. Turn out onto a sheet of plastic wrap, gather into a ball, then flatten into a 5-inch disk. Refrigerate for at least 30 minutes. Remove from the refrigerator 10 minutes before rolling out.

2. Roll the dough out on a lightly floured surface to an 11-inch circle. Ease into a 9-inch tart pan, trim the dough about ½ inch beyond the pan edges, turn the edges under, and press against the sides with your fingertips. Freeze the tart shell for at least 30 minutes. (Can be made up to 2 weeks ahead.)

3. Preheat the oven to 425°F/220°C.

4. Bake the tart shell, directly from the freezer, until lightly colored, 13 to 15 minutes. If the pastry starts to puff up, press the bottom gently with a large spatula or oven-mitted hand to flatten. Cool the shell while preparing the filling. Reduce the oven temperature to 350°F/180°C.

5. For the filling, whisk together the eggs, corn syrup, granulated sugar, and salt in a large bowl until blended. Whisk in →

the butter and vanilla. Stir in the pecans and chocolate chips. Pour into the cooled tart shell, distributing the nuts and chocolate chips more or less evenly.

6. Bake the tart in the preheated oven until the edges of the filling are firm when tested with the point of a small knife but the center is not completely set, 30 to 35 minutes. Cool on a rack. (Can be held at cool room temperature for up to 8 hours or refrigerated for up to a day or frozen for up to 3 weeks. Reheat in the oven at 350°F/180°C for about 15 minutes before serving.)

7. For the topping, whip the cream with the confectioners' sugar using an electric mixer until soft peaks form. Stir in the liqueur. (Can be made up to about 3 hours ahead and refrigerated.)

8. Serve the tart topped with dollops of the coffee cream.

LEMON SPONGE PUDDING CAKE

- 2 tablespoons unsalted butter, softened
- ¾ cup plus 1 tablespoon sugar
- 3 egg yolks
- ¼ cup all-purpose flour
- 1 tablespoon grated lemon zest
- ¼ cup fresh lemon juice
- 1¼ cups whole milk
- 4 egg whites
- ¼ teaspoon salt

A lemon dessert is just the ticket to complete many a chowder supper. This old-fashioned pudding cake, which separates magically into a top cake layer with a tangy lemon sauce underneath, is simple and fun to make and tastes absolutely scrumptious.

4–5 SERVINGS

1. Preheat the oven to 325°F/160°C. Butter a 1½-quart baking dish such as a soufflé dish.

2. Cream the butter and the ¾ cup sugar with an electric mixer in a medium bowl. Beat in the egg yolks and flour until well blended. Beat in the lemon zest and juice and whisk in the milk.

3. Beat the egg whites with the salt in a large bowl until foamy. Sprinkle on the remaining 1 tablespoon sugar and beat until soft peaks form. Pour the lemon mixture over the beaten egg whites and use a large whisk to stir gently, just until no lumps of egg white remain. Scrape the batter into the prepared dish. Place the baking dish in a larger pan and fill the pan to halfway up the sides of the pudding dish with boiling water. (It's easiest to do this while both pans are on the pulled-out oven rack.)

4. Bake in the preheated oven until the pudding top is a light golden brown and springs back when lightly touched, 25 to 30 minutes. Cool in the water bath for 20 minutes. Serve warm, room temperature, or chilled.

LATTICE-TOP BLUEBERRY PIE

This blueberry filling is as pure and pristine as a crisp, cloudless late summer day in Maine. It's best made with tiny, tart low-bush Maine berries, but if you're using fatter, highbush blueberries, you should decrease the sugar by a tablespoon or so to balance their sweetness. Blueberries are superbly complemented by an old-fashioned half-lard crust, and because they're such a pretty color, showcasing them with a woven lattice crust is definitely worth the bit of extra effort.

8–10 SERVINGS

CRUST

- 2½ cups all-purpose flour
- 2 teaspoons sugar
- 1 teaspoon salt
- ½ cup cold or frozen lard, cut into ½-inch chunks
- 6 tablespoons cold unsalted butter, cut into ½-inch slices or chunks
- 6–8 tablespoons ice water

FILLING

- ¾ cup sugar
- 3 tablespoons all-purpose flour
- ¼ teaspoon ground cinnamon
- ⅛ teaspoon salt
- 1 quart (about 4½ cups) fresh blueberries (see Note)
- 2 teaspoons fresh lemon juice
- 2 tablespoons unsalted butter, cut into pieces
- Vanilla ice cream, for serving (optional)

1. For the crust, combine the flour, sugar, and salt in a food processor and pulse to blend. Distribute the lard and butter over the flour and pulse until most of the shortening is about the size of peas. Sprinkle with 6 tablespoons of the ice water and pulse, stopping when the dough begins to clump together. If the mixture is too dry to press into a dough with your fingers, sprinkle on the remaining 1 to 2 tablespoons water and pulse a few more times. Turn the dough out onto two sheets of plastic wrap, gather into 2 balls, and flatten into 5-inch disks. Refrigerate for at least 30 minutes. Remove from the refrigerator 10 minutes before rolling out.

2. For the filling, stir together the sugar, flour, cinnamon, and salt in a large bowl. Add the blueberries and lemon juice and toss gently to combine. Set aside for 10 minutes to allow the berries to soften.

3. Preheat the oven to 425°F/220°C.

4. Roll one of the pastry disks out on a lightly floured surface to a 12-inch circle. Ease into a 9-inch pie plate. Roll out the second disk of pastry and use a ruler as a guide for cutting it into ¾-inch-wide strips.

5. Spoon the blueberry mixture into the pie shell and distribute the butter over the top.

6. Starting in the center, place the pastry strips over the filling, about ½ inch apart, and weave them over and under each other like a basket. Finish with the shorter strips. Trim the overhanging dough to about ½ inch all around and crimp or flute the edges to seal.

7. Bake in the preheated oven for 15 minutes. Reduce the oven temperature to 350°F/180°C and bake until the crust is a golden brown and the berry juices bubble through the lattice, 35 to 45 minutes. Cool on a wire rack. Serve slightly warm or at room temperature, topped with a scoop of ice cream if desired.

NOTE
Or you can use frozen berries. Thaw on paper towels for about 20 minutes before using.

PLUM-ALMOND GALETTE

I love the combination of summer fruits and almonds. When I happened across a Jacques Pepin recipe calling for a unique ground almond layer for a free-form tart, I worked out this adaptation thereof. Plums (any type) are delicious and beautiful here, but you can use almost any combination of other summer fruits, including berries, sliced peaches, nectarines, or apricots.

6–8 SERVINGS

PASTRY

- 1½ cups all-purpose flour
- ½ teaspoon salt
- 10 tablespoons cold unsalted butter, cut into about 12 pieces
- 4–6 tablespoons ice water

FILLING

- ⅓ cup sliced almonds, plus 2 tablespoons for the topping
- ¼ cup plus ⅓ cup sugar
- 2 tablespoons all-purpose flour
- 1 pound plums (any type), halved, pitted, and cut into ½-inch-thick slices (about 3 cups)
- 1 teaspoon fresh lemon juice
- 2 tablespoons unsalted butter, cut into small pieces
- 1 egg beaten with 2 teaspoons water
- Vanilla ice cream or lightly sweetened whipped cream, for serving

1. For the pastry, combine the flour and salt in a food processor and pulse to blend. Add the butter and pulse until the butter is about the size of peas. Sprinkle with 4 tablespoons of the ice water and pulse, stopping when the dough begins to clump together. If the mixture is too dry to press into a dough with your fingers, sprinkle on the remaining 1 to 2 tablespoons water and pulse a few more times. Turn the dough out onto a sheet of plastic wrap, gather into a ball, then flatten into a 5-inch disk. Refrigerate for at least 30 minutes. Remove from the refrigerator 10 minutes before rolling out.

2. Roll the dough out on a lightly floured surface into a 12-inch circle. Slide onto a rimmed parchment-lined baking sheet. (If not finishing the galette immediately, cover the dough loosely and refrigerate for up to 6 hours.)

3. Preheat the oven to 375°F/190°C.

4. For the filling, combine the ⅓ cup almonds, the ¼ cup sugar, and the flour in a food processor and process until the almonds are ground fine. Spread the mixture evenly over the dough round to within about 2½ inches of the edge.

5. Toss the plums with the remaining ⅓ cup sugar and the lemon juice, arrange over the almond mixture, and dot with the butter. Fold the edges of the dough up over the plums, pleating as necessary to create a rough 2-inch border. ⊙

Brush the border with the beaten egg and sprinkle with the 2 tablespoons of sliced almonds.

6. Bake in the preheated oven until the pastry is a rich golden brown and the fruit is soft and the juices bubbly, 50 minutes to 1 hour. Use a large spatula to transfer to a wire rack to cool. (Can be made several hours ahead and held at cool room temperature.)

7. Serve warm or at room temperature, with scoops of ice cream or whipped cream.

BLACK PEPPER BROWNIES

Brownies — especially fudgy ones like these — can sometimes be too sweet, but the black pepper in this recipe balances the sugar nicely and gives the brownies an interesting, sophisticated edge. They'd be a welcome finish to any chowder or seafood stew supper.

MAKES 16–20 BROWNIES

½ cup (1 stick) unsalted butter

2 ounces unsweetened chocolate, coarsely chopped

2 eggs

1 cup sugar

1 teaspoon vanilla extract

½ teaspoon salt

¼ teaspoon black pepper

½ cup chopped walnuts

½ cup all-purpose flour

1. Preheat the oven to 350°F/180°C. Butter an 8- or 9-inch square baking pan.

2. Melt the butter with the chocolate over medium-low heat in a medium saucepan.

3. Whisk the eggs with the sugar, vanilla, salt, and pepper in a large bowl. Gradually whisk in the chocolate mixture and stir in the walnuts. Sift the flour over the chocolate mixture and whisk gently just until no specks of flour remain. Scrape into the prepared pan.

4. Bake in the preheated oven until a tester inserted two-thirds of the way into the center comes out clean, 25 to 30 minutes. Cool in the pan for about 20 minutes and then cut into 16 to 20 squares or rectangles. Serve immediately, store in the refrigerator for up to 2 days, or freeze.

SOUR LEMON TART
in a GRAHAM CRACKER CRUST

A zest-packed lemon curd nestles in a sweet graham cracker crust and is topped with a thin layer of whipped cream, making for a beautiful and scrumptious tart. It's just the ticket to complete almost any chowder meal, but especially a spicy chowder or stew such as Creole Seafood Gumbo (page 72).

8 SERVINGS

CRUST

- 7 whole graham crackers, broken into pieces
- 4 tablespoons unsalted butter, melted
- 3 tablespoons granulated sugar

FILLING AND TOPPING

- 2 eggs
- 6 egg yolks
- 1 cup granulated sugar
- Pinch of salt
- ¼ cup grated lemon zest (see Notes)
- ½ cup fresh lemon juice
- ½ cup (1 stick) unsalted butter, cut into several pieces
- ½ cup heavy cream
- 1 tablespoon confectioners' sugar
- 1 very thin lemon slice

1. Preheat the oven to 325°F/160°C.

2. For the crust, process the graham crackers in a food processor to make fine, even crumbs, about 30 seconds. You should have 1 cup of crumbs. Sprinkle the butter and granulated sugar over the crumbs and pulse to blend. Turn out into a 9- to 9½-inch tart pan with a removable bottom. Use the bottom of a glass to press the crumbs into an even layer on the bottom of the pan and bring them most of the way up the sides.

3. Bake in the preheated oven until the crust is fragrant and barely begins to brown, 12 to 15 minutes. Cool on a wire rack. (Can be made a day ahead. Cover and refrigerate.)

4. When you're ready to make the filling, preheat the oven to 350°F/180°C.

5. For the filling, whisk the eggs, yolks, granulated sugar, and salt in a medium nonreactive saucepan (see Note), then whisk in the lemon zest and juice. Place the pan over medium-low heat. Add the butter and cook, whisking constantly, until the butter melts, steam rises, and the mixture thickens into a moderately thick lemon curd, about 5 minutes. Pour the warm filling into the cooled crust. ⊙

6. Bake in the preheated oven until the top is pale golden brown and the edges are set but the center still jiggles when gently shaken, 20 to 25 minutes. Cool on a wire rack and refrigerate until ready to add the topping. (Can be made to this point several hours ahead.)

7. For the topping, whip the cream with the confectioners' sugar until stiff peaks form. Spread the cream over the top of the tart and place the lemon slice in the center. (Can be made 2 to 3 hours ahead and refrigerated.)

8. Remove the tart from the pan and place on a serving platter. Cut into wedges to serve.

NOTES
Aluminum or cast-iron pans can turn the egg mixture a greenish color. Any other material is fine.

You will need 3 to 4 lemons for this amount of zest and juice. Zest the lemons (colder lemons grate better) before squeezing out the juice.

OVERSIZE OATMEAL-RAISIN COOKIES

A plate of old-fashioned raisin-studded oatmeal cookies is just the thing to complete a meal of any of the classic chowders, such as Boston-Style Creamy Clam Chowder (page 9). This recipe is based on one in *The Cook's Illustrated Cookbook*, one of the most reliable references around.

MAKES 14 LARGE COOKIES

¾ cup all-purpose flour

½ teaspoon baking powder

¼ teaspoon salt

¼ teaspoon ground cinnamon

¼ teaspoon grated nutmeg

½ cup (1 stick) unsalted butter, softened

½ cup firmly packed light brown sugar

½ cup granulated sugar

1 egg

1½ cups old-fashioned or quick rolled oats (not instant oatmeal)

¾ cup raisins

1. Preheat the oven to 350°F/180°C. Line two baking sheets with parchment paper.

2. Whisk the flour with the baking powder, salt, cinnamon, and nutmeg in a medium bowl.

3. Combine the butter with the brown sugar and granulated sugar in a large bowl and mix with an electric mixer until well creamed. Add the egg and beat until smooth. With the mixer on low speed, add the flour mixture and the oats and beat until well blended. Stir in the raisins.

4. Using a 3-tablespoon cookie scoop, make balls of dough and drop about 2 inches apart on the prepared baking sheets. (Or chill the dough and roll 2-inch balls of dough by hand.)

5. Bake in the preheated oven, rotating the baking sheets front to back halfway through the baking time, until the cookies are pale golden brown around the edges but still soft and light colored in the center, 17 to 20 minutes. Cool for a couple of minutes on the baking sheets and transfer to a wire rack to cool completely. Store in a covered container for up to 3 days or freeze.

STRAWBERRY-RHUBARB COBBLER

FRUIT LAYER

- 2½ cups hulled and sliced strawberries
- 2½ cups chopped rhubarb
- ½ cup sugar
- ½ teaspoon grated orange zest
- 2 teaspoons fresh lemon juice
- 1 teaspoon vanilla extract

DOUGH

- 1 cup all-purpose flour
- 1 tablespoon cornmeal
- 2 teaspoons baking powder
- ½ teaspoon salt
- ¼ cup sugar plus 1 teaspoon for sprinkling on top
- 5 tablespoons cold unsalted butter, cut into about 10 pieces
- ⅓ cup whole or low-fat milk
  Lightly sweetened whipped cream or vanilla ice cream, for serving

A cobbler is such a wonderful way to showcase spring and summer fruits of all kinds. I have worked out the proportions of this recipe carefully so that the amount of biscuit topping is just right — not too cakey — for a one-quart dish. Its sweetness is pegged to the strawberry and rhubarb filling, so if you use very ripe, sweet fruit, you might want to decrease the sugar by a tablespoon or two. A hint of cornmeal adds a pleasing, slightly gritty texture to the cobbler dough.

4–6 SERVINGS

1. Preheat the oven to 400°F/200°C. Generously butter a shallow 1-quart baking dish such as a deep pie plate or 8-inch square dish.

2. Toss the strawberries and rhubarb with the sugar, orange zest, lemon juice, and vanilla in the prepared baking dish. Bake in the preheated oven for 10 minutes. Stir before adding the topping.

3. For the dough, combine the flour, cornmeal, baking powder, salt, and ¼ cup sugar in a food processor and pulse to blend. Distribute the butter over the flour mixture and pulse until the butter is about the size of peas. Slowly pour the

milk through the feed tube, pulsing until the dough begins to clump together. (To make by hand, whisk together the dry ingredients in a large bowl, work the butter in with your fingertips until the butter is about the size of peas, and add the milk all at once and stir with a fork.)

4. Transfer the dough to a lightly floured board, knead a few times to bring the dough together, and roll or pat out into a shape a bit smaller than the top of the dish. Either crimp the edges and place the dough over the fruit or cut into rounds, squares, or triangles and arrange atop the fruit. If you're using one large piece of dough, cut several deep slashes to let steam escape. Sprinkle with the remaining 1 teaspoon sugar.

5. Bake until the topping is golden and the fruit is bubbly, 20 to 30 minutes. Serve warm or at room temperature, with whipped cream or ice cream.

CRANBERRY-APPLE UPSIDE-DOWN CAKE

This cake combines ruby-red cranberries and apple slices to make the gorgeous glistening topping. The cake layer is an eggy sponge enriched with ground walnuts and a tiny bit of cornmeal for that pleasant crumbly texture. Tie the whole together with apple brandy–spiked whipped cream and serve as the finish to a fall or winter chowder supper.

8 SERVINGS

FRUIT LAYER

- 1¼ cups cranberries
- ½ cup granulated sugar
- ½ cup water
- 1 firm sweet apple, such as Golden Delicious, cored, peeled, and thinly sliced
- 4 tablespoons unsalted butter, cut into several pieces

CAKE

- ¾ cup all-purpose flour
- 2 teaspoons cornmeal
- ¾ teaspoon baking powder
- ½ teaspoon salt
- ¼ teaspoon ground cinnamon
- ¼ cup coarsely chopped walnuts
- 3 eggs
- ¾ cup granulated sugar
- 1 teaspoon vanilla extract

TOPPING

- 1 cup heavy cream
- ¼ cup confectioners' sugar
- 2 tablespoons apple brandy, other apple liqueur, or plain brandy

1. For the fruit layer, combine the cranberries, granulated sugar, and water in a large saucepan. Bring to a boil, then reduce the heat to low and cook, covered, until the berries pop, 8 to 10 minutes. The sauce should have some syrupy juices; if it is too thick, add a couple tablespoons of water.

2. Add the apple and cook for 1 minute. Add the butter and stir until it melts. Scrape into a 9-inch cake pan and set aside to cool for at least 10 minutes.

3. Preheat the oven to 350°F/180°C.

4. For the cake, combine the flour, cornmeal, baking powder, salt, and cinnamon in a medium bowl and whisk to blend. Combine the walnuts in a food processor with about 1 tablespoon of the flour mixture and process until finely ground. Add to the flour mixture.

5. Using an electric mixer, beat the eggs with the sugar in a large bowl until light and nearly tripled in volume, about 3 minutes. Beat in the vanilla. With the mixer on low speed, add the flour mixture and beat just until blended. Pour the batter over the cranberry-apple layer.

6. Bake in the preheated oven until the cake springs back when touched in the center and a tester inserted in the center comes out clean, 30 to 35 minutes. Cool in the pan for 5 minutes. Run a paring knife around the edge of the cake and immediately invert onto a serving platter. Leave the pan on the cake for a few minutes, then lift it off. If any topping clings to the pan, simply transfer it to the top of the cake. (Can be made several hours ahead and held at room temperature.)

7. For the topping, whip the cream with the sugar and brandy to soft peaks. Serve the cake at room temperature, topped with the whipped cream.

DARK and STICKY CANDIED GINGERBREAD

GINGERBREAD

1¾ cups all-purpose flour

¼ teaspoon salt

1½ teaspoons baking soda

1½ teaspoons ground ginger

1 teaspoon ground cinnamon

½ teaspoon grated nutmeg

¼ teaspoon ground cloves

½ cup molasses

½ cup dark corn syrup

½ cup firmly packed dark brown sugar

6 tablespoons unsalted butter

¾ cup orange juice

¼ cup finely chopped candied ginger

2 eggs

SHERRIED FOAMY SAUCE

½ cup (1 stick) unsalted butter, softened

⅔ cup confectioners' sugar

½ cup boiling water

¼ cup sweet sherry or Madeira

1 egg, lightly beaten

Melanie Barnard (my coauthor on several books) and I once listed our requirements for the ultimate gingerbread cake. We agreed that it should be moist almost to the point of stickiness, dark with molasses, fragrant with spice, and maybe freshened with just a hint of citrus. This cake, which we developed after more than a few trials and errors, is the result. The chopped candied ginger is not absolutely essential but it lifts this cake from excellent to extraordinary. Serve it after an autumn or winter chowder supper in a pool of this sherried foamy sauce, or simply top with a scoop of vanilla ice cream.

8 SERVINGS

1. Preheat the oven to 350°F/180°C. Butter a 9-inch square baking pan. If you're planning to unmold the cake and present it whole, line the bottom with parchment paper.

2. For the gingerbread, whisk together the flour, salt, baking soda, ginger, cinnamon, nutmeg, and cloves in a large bowl.

3. Combine the molasses, corn syrup, brown sugar, and butter in a medium saucepan. Bring to a boil over medium-high heat, stirring frequently, until the butter melts and the mixture is smooth and bubbly. Remove from the heat, stir in the orange juice and candied ginger, and let cool for 5 minutes. Whisk in the eggs. ⟳

4. Make a well in the center of the flour mixture, add the molasses mixture, and whisk or beat on low speed with an electric mixer until smooth. (The batter will be foamy and quite thin.) Pour into the prepared pan.

5. Bake in the center of the preheated oven until a toothpick inserted in the center comes out clean, 30 to 35 minutes.

6. Cool in the pan on a wire rack. Serve warm or at room temperature, cut into squares, plain or in a pool of the sherried foamy sauce. (The gingerbread can be stored, covered, in the refrigerator for up to a day or frozen.)

7. For the sauce, cream the butter with the confectioners' sugar in a metal bowl until smooth. (The recipe can be made ahead to this step.) Shortly before serving, whisk the boiling water and sherry into the butter mixture. Whisk in the egg. Place the bowl over a saucepan of simmering water and whisk until the sauce thickens slightly and is foamy, about 5 minutes. Serve immediately.

SPICED HERMIT BAR COOKIES

Fragrant with sweet spices and studded with raisins and walnuts, this dessert is a lovely old-fashioned bar cookie that goes very well with such classic chowders as Connecticut Shoreline Semi-Clear Clam Chowder (page 11) and Vineyard Chicken and Corn Chowder (page 52).

MAKES ABOUT 24 BARS

1 cup all-purpose flour
½ teaspoon baking powder
½ teaspoon baking soda
¼ teaspoon ground cinnamon
¼ teaspoon grated nutmeg
⅛ teaspoon ground cloves
½ teaspoon salt
5 tablespoons unsalted butter, softened
¼ cup sugar
1 egg
¼ cup molasses
½ cup raisins, coarsely chopped
½ cup walnuts, chopped

1. Preheat the oven to 350°F/180°C. Grease an 8-inch square baking pan.

2. Whisk together the flour, baking powder, baking soda, cinnamon, nutmeg, cloves, and salt in a medium bowl.

3. Using an electric mixer, beat the butter with the sugar in a large bowl until light and fluffy. Add the egg and molasses and beat until smooth. Add the flour mixture and beat on very low speed until blended, or mix in with a wooden spoon. Stir in the raisins and nuts. Scrape the batter, which will be quite stiff, into the prepared pan and spread it out fairly evenly, smoothing the top.

4. Bake in the preheated oven until the edges are lightly browned and a tester inserted in the center comes out clean, 15 to 18 minutes. Cool in the pan on a rack before cutting into 1½- to 2-inch bars. Store in a tightly covered container for up to 3 days or freeze.

INDEX

Page numbers in *italic* indicate photos.

CONVERTING RECIPE MEASUREMENTS to METRIC

Use the following formulas for converting U.S. measurements to metric. Since the conversions are not exact, it's important to convert the measurements for all of the ingredients to maintain the same proportions as the original recipe.

WHEN THE MEASUREMENT GIVEN IS	MULTIPLY IT BY	TO CONVERT TO
teaspoons	4.93	milliliters
tablespoons	14.79	milliliters
fluid ounces	29.57	milliliters
cups	236.59	milliliters
cups	0.236	liters
pints	473.18	milliliters
pints	0.473	liters
quarts	946.36	milliliters
quarts	0.946	liters
gallons	3.785	liters
ounces	28.35	grams
pounds	0.454	kilograms
inches	2.54	centimeters